101
4-3 STUNTS

Leo Hand

COACHES CHOICE™

ISBN: 1-58518-593-0
Library of Congress Catalog Card Number: 2001098594

Book design: Jeanne Hamilton
Diagrams: Rebecca Gold Rubin
Cover design: Bean Creek Studio
Front cover photo: Craig Jones/Getty Images

Coaches Choice
P.O. Box 1828
Monterey, CA 93942
www.coacheschoice.com

DEDICATION

For two beautiful ladies named Mary.

ACKNOWLEDGMENTS

Thanks to my wife, Mary, for urging me to follow my heart and return to *big-city coaching* even though it involved sacrifice for her.

Thanks to Raina for the adjustments she had to make.

Thanks to Tony Shaw for giving me the opportunity to coach in Texas.

Thanks to Jim Murphy for all he taught me about defense at Long Beach City College.

Thanks to the wonderful people of the Zuni and Navajo Nations who taught me much more than I taught them during the seven years I lived with them.

Thanks to Joe Griffin for giving me one of the best coaching jobs in California.

Thanks to all of the splendid young men whom I have been privileged to coach.

Thanks to all of the great coaches whom I have been fortunate to have worked with and coached against.

Thanks to Phil Johnson for all of his help and kind words.

Thanks to Conrado Ronquillo and the maintenance crew at Irvin High School for all of their patience, kindness, and help during this project.

Thanks to the offspring whose ancestors endured the *Middle Chamber* and the *Long Walk* for all of the contributions that they have made to the greatest game of all.

Thanks to Howard Wells for giving me the opportunity to coach at El Paso High.

Thanks to Herman L. Masin, Editor-in-Chif of Scholastic Coach for all of his help and suggestions during the past 30 years.

Thanks to Dr. James A. Peterson for all of his help during this project.

CONTENTS

ATTENTION: WE ARE NOW PLAYING THE GAME BY NEW RULES

The old football adage, *live by the blitz, die by the blitz* is as outdated as leather helmets, handlebar moustaches, and fat footballs without stripes. The zone blitz, one of the most innovative and exciting defensive strategies to ever arrive on the football scene, is presently rewriting the rules of how the game is to be played.

The zone blitz limits the number of receivers an offense can put into a pass pattern and safely protect its quarterback by taking away hot reads and holding the offense accountable for blocking seven or eight defenders in the box. This objective is accomplished by a tactic called *illusion*. At the snap of the ball, seven or eight defenders will attack the line of scrimmage and give the offense the *illusion* of a *total blitz*. Once the defense read pass; however, only four pre-determined defenders will continue to rush the quarterback. The remaining three or four *fake blitzers* will drop off into coverage. To compound the offensive problem even further, the *fake blitzers* may be defensive linemen. The offense therefore never knows (until it is too late) how *many* and *which* defenders will rush the quarterback. In the *old days*, the defenders who lined up in three-point stances were pass rushers, and the players who lined up in two-point stances were either pass rushers (if they blitzed) or coverage players. Today, every player aligned in the box is both a potential pass rusher and a coverage player. The zone blitz has therefore rewritten the rules of pass protection by creating a chaotic guessing game for the offense.

The zone blitz is also deadly versus the run because the seven or eight defenders in the box are attacking and penetrating the line of scrimmage, and the secondary is reading the ball and backing up the defenders in the box rather than being locked onto a receiver. If in future years, offensive teams try to counter the zone blitz by employing formations that feature no running backs, they will become one dimensional and whenever an offense become one dimensional, it becomes easy to defend.

This book includes not only zone blitzing strategies but also a multitude of other blitzing tactics that enable the defense to truly attack the offense. Whether you've decided to *live by the blitz*, or you simply want to augment your present 4-3 package with a few innovative ideas, this book will serve as a valuable resource for years to come.

WHICH 4-3?

When I decided to write a book about 4-3 stunts, the first question that I had to ask myself was "which 4-3?" It's almost mind boggling the number of variations of the

4-3 that coaches have developed in recent years. After carefully considering this question, I finally decided that I'd try to include as many variations as possible. I concluded that most 4-3 coaches, even the most conservative ones, are using quite a few variations in their defensive package, and if I were to settle on only one variation, I may satisfy a handful of coaches, but most would feel short-changed. So, as you page through this book, you will see stunts illustrated from variations of a balanced pro 4-3, variations of a balanced college 4-3, and variations of an unbalanced overloaded 4-3 (which many coaches refer to as a *reduction* or a *load*). You'll also occasionally see defensive linemen lined up in a tilt or flexed position. Hopefully, this approach will provide new ideas for all coaches and stimulate innovative thinking. I'm also sure that any coach who may be interested in a specific stunt, but not interested in the front from which it's illustrated, will have no difficulty adapting the stunt to a 4-3 variation of his liking.

I also didn't name any of the stunts or fronts. Because each coach has his own unique nomenclature, it seemed senseless to bore a reader with mine. Besides, most coaches who read this book will be looking for innovative ideas, not an entirely new system.

There are a few terms that I will be constantly referring to as I explain the stunts. Because I do not want to assume (ass-u-me) anything, these terms are defined before the text begins.

- Strongside/weakside: The strongside is toward the tight end, and the weakside is toward the split end. Strong defenders (example: strong tackle) are aligned on the tight-end side, and weak defenders are aligned on the split-end side.

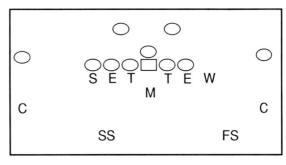

- Player positions will be referred to by the following names:

Strong cornerback— the cornerback who lines up opposite the flanker.	Free safety— the safety who lines up toward the split-end side.
Strong safety— the safety who lines up toward the tight-end side.	Sam—the outside linebacker who lines up on the strongside.

Strong end— the defensive end who lines up on the strongside.	Weak tackle—the defensive tackle who lines up on the weakside.
Strong tackle— the defensive tackle who lines up on the strongside.	Weak end— the defensive end who lines up on the weakside.
Mike— the middle linebacker.	Will— the outside linebacker who lines up on the weakside.

• Gap responsibilities will be given the following letter designations:

D   C   B   A   A   B   C   D

• Alignment numbering system will be as follows:

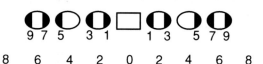

9 7 5   3 1   1 3   5 7 9

8   6   4   2   0   2   4   6   8

Even numbers are head up (except 8)
Odd numbers are inside/outside shade

• Pro 4-3: is a 4-3 variation in which the strong end aligns in a 5 technique and the Sam aligns in a 9 technique.

S   E   T   T   E   W

M

• College 4-3: is a 4-3 variation in which the strong end will align in a 7 or 9 technique, and Sam will align in a flexed 5 or 7 technique. Frequently, the weak end will line up in a 7 technique and Will will line up in a flexed 4 technique.

E   T   T   E

S   M   W

- Reduction/load or overload: Four defenders will line up toward the strongside, and three defenders will line up on the weakside. There are many variations of this. The following diagram illustrates four examples:

"Load" or "Reduction" alignments

- Over: is a variation of the 4-3 in which the weak tackle and Mike switch positions.

"Over" variation of a Pro 4-3

- Under: is a variation of the 4-3 in which Mike and the strong tackle switch positions.

"Under" variation of a Pro 4-3

- Over read: A linebacker is assigned to read backfield flow.

- Under read: A linebacker is assigned to read backfield flow *through* an offensive lineman.

CHAPTER 1

BASIC PRINCIPLES
OF BLITZING

- If you use the blitz as an element of surprise and do it infrequently, it's important that you disguise your intention.

- If you frequently blitz, disguising your intention may not be as important because you may want to occasionally give the offense a false key by *showing blitz* but then *playing straight* at the snap of the ball. Whatever you decide, it is important that you do not establish a pattern that becomes a key that can be exploited.

- Your eyes are one of your most important tools when blitzing. To be an effective blitzer, you must be able to see (on the run) the keys that that will lead you to the ball. Seeing these keys is the first step in being able to read and react to them.

- Unless the blitz is a delayed reaction to a pass, it is critical that you're moving, attacking, and penetrating the line of scrimmage at the snap of the ball.

- Keep your feet moving at all times. This factor is especially important when you become engaged with a blocker.

- Use your quickness in an attempt to avoid blockers.

- If the play is a pass, and you become engaged with a blocker, keep your hands inside of the blocker's hands and try to maintain separation from the blocker. Do not look at the passer too soon and lose sight of the blocker. You must first defeat the blocker before you can sack the quarterback. Have a predetermined pass rush move in mind but be ready to change your move according to the circumstance. Take what the blocker gives you and make your move at the appropriate time. Remember that if you make your pass rush move too soon, the blocker will have time to recover. On the other hand, if you make your move too late, you will probably be too close to the blocker, and he will be able to get into your body and nullify your charge. If possible, try to get the blocker turned one way and then make your move in the opposite direction. Also, use your forward momentum to manipulate the blocker's momentum. If the blocker's momentum is back, attack him with a power move and knock him backwards. If his momentum is forward, use a move that puts him forward and destroys his balance. Lastly, never leave your feet to bat a ball down. Get your hands up as the quarterback begins his throwing motion but keep charging toward the quarterback. Too often when a defender jumps up to bat a pass down, the quarterback will duck under, allude the defender, and scramble out of the pocket.

- If the play is a run, react to your keys and the pressure of blocks as you normally would if you were employing a read technique. Since you have forward momentum to your advantage, use your hands rather than your forearm when attacking a blocker. Maintain separation from blockers and don't let them get into your legs. If possible, make the blocker miss you.

- Keep your body under control at all times and try to maintain a low center of gravity. Provide a small target for blockers.

- Study your opponents' game films carefully. Know how potential blockers react and what techniques they favor. Know their strengths and weaknesses.

- Study your opponents eyes as they're getting set at the line of scrimmage. Their eyes will often tell you where they're going. Also study the pressure that they put on their down hand when they get into their stances. You can frequently find a player who will give you a pass/run or a directional key by the pressure he puts on his down hand.

- Study the scouting report. Know your opponents' formation, down-and-distance, and field position tendency. Use this information to anticipate, but never to guess.

- Gang tackle, and if possible try to strip the ball out of the ballcarier's arm. Never take for granted that a running back or quarterback has been downed. If you arrive at a pile late, be on the alert for a loose ball.

- Maintain total intensity from the time the ball is snapped until the whistle is blown.

- Before the snap, anticipate potential blockers and be prepared to react to these blockers as you penetrate the line.

- On plays directed toward your side of the line, you should make the tackle. On plays directed away from you, take the proper angle of pursuit and be in on the tackle. Always pursue relentlessly. Remember that if you are not within five yards of the ball when the whistle blows, you are probably loafing.

- If the backfield action does not indicate flow, protect your gap until you find the ball. Do not guess.

- If you're assigned to *spy* (cover a back) when you're blitzing, expect that the back will first block and then run a delayed route. Do not be fooled. Remember that you must cover the back until the whistle blows no matter what he does.

- The ball is you trigger. When the ball is snapped, *you're gone!* Do not listen to an opponent's cadence; they're not talking to you!

- Do not rely upon the lines that are marked on the field. The ball, not the lines, establishes the line of scrimmage.

CHAPTER 2

ZERO COVERAGE STUNTS

When Zero Coverage is employed, three defensive backs will be assigned to guard a receiver man-to-man and the fourth defensive back will usually (but not always) be sent on a blitz. This chapter presents the following five variations of Zero Coverage:

- Zero Coverage that employs a free safety blitz

- Zero Coverage that employs a strong safety blitz.

- Zero Coverage that employs an overload blitz (four blitzers on one side of the ball) or a fake overload.

- Zero Coverage that employs a weak cornerback blitz.

- Zero coverage in which the free safety or strong safety fakes a blitz and covers the near back.

The strength of Zero Coverage is that it has eight defenders in the vicinity of the box attacking the gaps and penetrating the line of scrimmage. Its weakness is that all secondary defenders are locked on receivers and none are keying the ball; therefore, if a run breaks the line of scrimmage or a defensive back gets beat deep, a good chance exists that a touchdown will result.

Despite its weakness, Zero Coverage can cause an offense a lot of problems, especially when the defenders in the box have some *quicks* and the defensive backs are skillful man-to-man pass defenders. I recently heard an very successful coach, Allen Wilson from John Tyler High School in Tyler, Texas, give an excellent talk at a coaching clinic. Zero coverage is Coach Wilson's predominate pass coverage, and John Tyler High School is a perennial state contender. In his presentation, Coach Wilson reasoned that Zero coverage is not as risky as it may seem because even the finest passing teams usually have only one or two excellent pass receivers.

A defense will therefore need only one or two very talented defensive backs to cover these receivers. He also pointed out that the intense pressure that a well-thought out Zero Coverage blitz package puts on an offense often offsets the ability of a good quarterback and his receivers.

Another exceptional coach, Dan Markhan, who is one of the finest high school coaches in America today, takes Zero Coverage to the limit. Coach Markham uses a lot of Zero coverage and employs both of his Cornerbacks to play bump and run with no help deep. By doing this, the timing between the quarterback and his receivers is not only disrupted, but the variety of pass routes that a opponent can sensibly throw versus this technique becomes very limited. I've been privileged to play coach Markham's teams in the past, and about the only patterns that we were able to throw were fades, comebacks, corners, and post/corners – that is when we had time to throw.

ILLUSION STUNTS

At the beginning of this chapter, quite a few *illusion stunts* are covered. Illusion stunts are the predecessor of the zone blitz. I started using *illusion stunts* in the '80's and had a great deal of success with them. I call this category of stunts *illusion stunts* because they give the offense the *illusion* of a seven-or eight-man rush. At the snap of the ball, seven or eight defenders will attack the line. Two of these defenders will not penetrate the line; instead, they will draw offensive blocks, and then *spy* (cover the two running backs) if a pass develops. If the play is a run, the two *spy* defenders will defend their assigned gap and play run. Often the two defenders assigned to *spy* the backs are defensive linemen. This step may sound risky, but in reality it's not. Illusion stunts hold the offense accountable for blocking all seven or eight defenders in the box. This factor means that the offense can only send out two or three receivers and still adequately protect their quarterback (remember, the offense never knows which two defenders are spying the backs).

In almost twenty years of using illusion stunts, about the only two patterns that I've ever seen completed to the backs were delays and screens, and these completions resulted because the defender assigned to *spy* lost his concentration and didn't stay with his assigned back. The quarterback simply doesn't have time to complete any other patterns to his backs. It is vital that coaches who decide to employ illusion stunts, stress discipline and concentration in teaching the *spy* technique.

STUNT #1

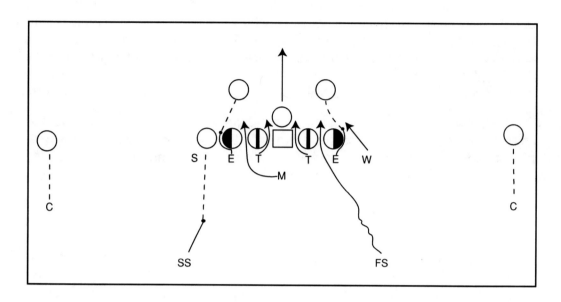

COACHING POINTS:

- This blitz is illustrated from **zero coverage** that features a **free Safety Blitz**. The secondary is disguised as 2 zone.

- The front is a balanced variation of the pro 4-3.

- This is an **illusion stunt** that gives the offense the *illusion* that eight defenders are blitzing.

- The free safety and Mike are blitzing the B gaps. Both Sam and Will are on a contained rush. The two ends are aligned in 5 techniques; they are both responsible for controlling the C gap and *spying* the two running backs. The two tackles are aligned in 2 techniques, and they are both slanting into the A gaps. Since it is impossible for a standard protection scheme to protect the quarterback, the quarterback will not have enough time to complete a normal pattern to either of the backs. The two ends must therefore be particularly conscious of covering either a screen or delayed route to their assigned back.

- The defenders filling gaps are responsible for cutback.

STUNT #2

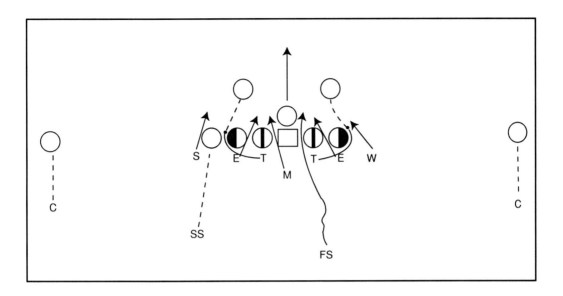

COACHING POINTS:

- This stunt, which features a **free safety blitz**, is illustrated from a variation of **zero coverage** that is disguised as 3 sky.

- The front is a balanced variation of the pro 4-3.

- This is an **illusion stunt** that gives the offense the *illusion* of an eight-man blitz.

- The free safety and Mike are blitzing the A gaps. Both Sam and Will are on a contained rush. The ends and tackles are twisting. The two tackles are responsible for *spying* the running backs. The twist between the tackles and ends should occur immediately as the ball is snapped.

- The defenders filling the gaps are responsible for cutback.

STUNT #3

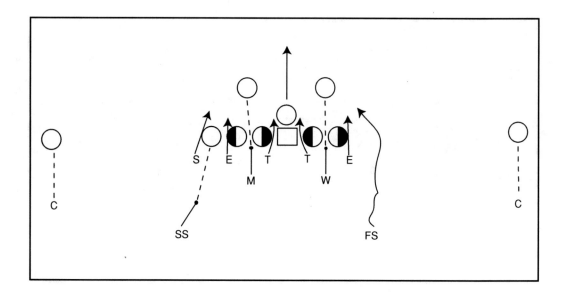

COACHING POINTS:

- This **free safety blitz** is illustrated from a variation of **zero coverage** that is disguised as 2 zone.

- The front is an unbalanced variation of an overloaded 4-3.

- This is an **illusion stunt** that gives the offense the *illusion* of an eight-man blitz

- The free safety is blitzing the D gap and is on a contained rush. Sam is also on a contained rush. Both Mike and Will are faking blitzes through the B gaps and are assigned to *spy* the near backs. The two tackles are both aligned in 2 techniques; they are both slanting into the A gaps.

- When flow goes away from Mike or Will, he should fold back and pursue laterally watching for cutback.

STUNT #4

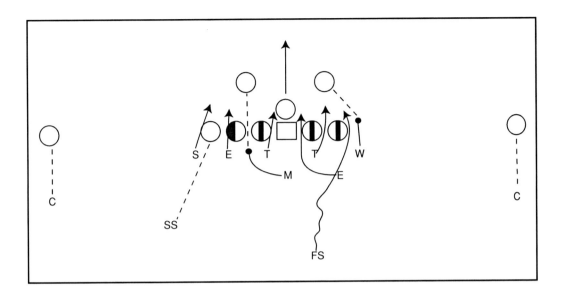

COACHING POINTS:

- This **free safety blitz** is illustrated from a variation of **zero coverage** that is disguised as 3 sky.

- The front is a balanced variation of the pro 4-3 in which the weak end is aligned in a flexed 6 technique.

- This is an **illusion stunt** that gives the offense the *illusion* of an eight-man blitz.

- The free safety is blitzing the C gap, and is responsible for containment versus pass, but not run. Weakside run containment is Will's responsibility. Will is also responsible for *spying* the near back. The weak end and weak tackle are twisting. Mike is faking a blitz through the B gap and is assigned to *spy* the near back. Sam is aligned up in a 9 technique; he is responsible for strong side containment. The strong end is aligned in a 5 technique and is responsible for controlling the C gap. The strong tackle is aligned in a 2 technique and slanting into the A gap.

- When flow goes away from Mike or Will, he should fold back and pursue laterally, watching for cutback.

STUNT #5

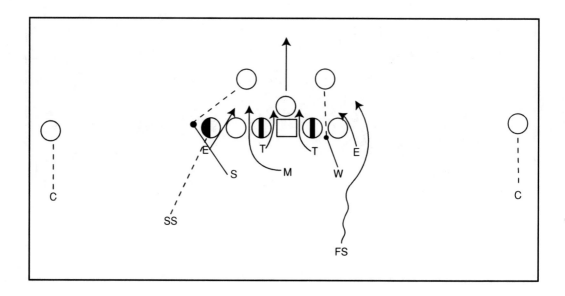

COACHING POINTS:

- This **free safety blitz** is illustrated from a variation of **zero coverage** that is disguised as 3 sky.

- The front is a balanced variation of the college 4-3.

- This is an **illusion stunt** that gives the offense the *illusion* of an eight-man blitz.

- The free safety is blitzing the D gap, and is responsible for containment versus both pass and run. The weak end is aligned in a 7 technique; he is slanting toward the outside heel of the offensive tackle and is responsible for controlling the C gap. Will is faking a blitz into the B gap and spying the near back. Sam and the strong end are twisting. This twist should occur immediately as the ball is snapped. The strong end is responsible for containment versus the pass and controlling the C gap versus run. Sam is responsible for strongside containment versus the run and *spying* the back versus pass. Both tackles are slanting into the A gaps.

- When flow goes away from Sam or Will, he should fold back and pursue laterally watching for cutback.

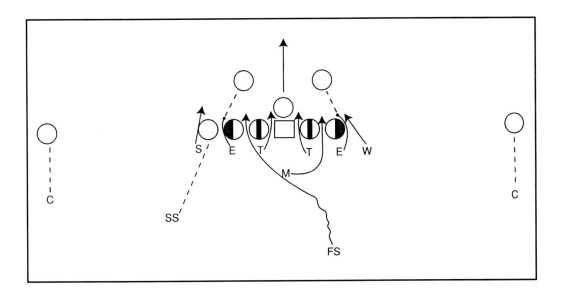

COACHING POINTS:

- This **free safety Blitz** is illustrated from a variation of **zero coverage** that is disguised as 3 sky.

- The front is a balanced variation of the pro 4-3.

- This is an **illusion stunt** that gives the offense the *illusion* of an eight-man blitz.

- The two tackles are slanting into the A gaps. The free safety is blitzing the strongside B gap, and Mike is blitzing the weakside B gap. Both Sam and Will are on a contained rush. Both ends are aligned in 5 techniques; they are responsible for controlling the C gap and *spying* the near backs.

- The defenders filling the gaps are responsible for cutback.

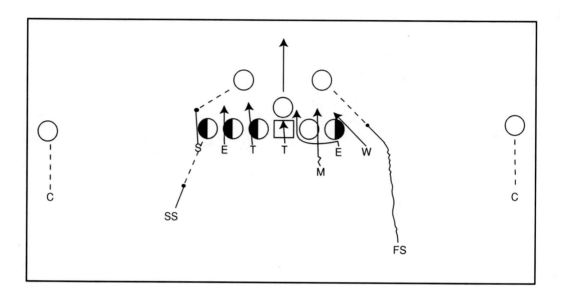

COACHING POINTS:

- This **fake free safety blitz** is illustrated from a variation of **zero coverage** that is disguised as 2 zone.

- The front is a balanced (*over*) variation of a pro 4-3.

- This is an **illusion stunt** that gives the offense the *illusion* of an eight-man blitz.

- Sam will line up in a 9 technique, control the D gap, and *spy* the near back. The strong end will line up in a 5 technique and control the C gap. The strong tackle will line up in a 3 technique and control the B gap. The weak tackle will line up in a 0 technique and control the strongside A gap. Mike will *show blitz* and blitz through the outside shoulder of the offensive guard. The weak end will draw the offensive tackle's block and then loop into the weakside A gap. Will will slant hard through the offensive tackle's outside shoulder, control the C gap, and contain the passer. The free safety will fake an outside blitz, contain weak side runs, and *spy* the near back.

- The free safety and Sam are responsible for cutback.

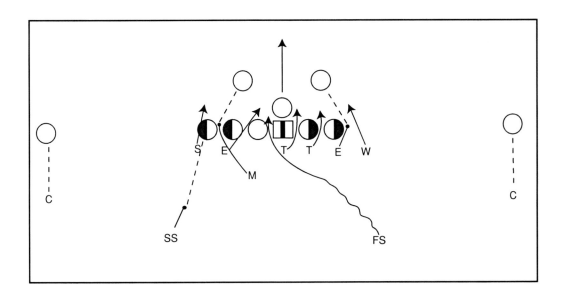

COACHING POINTS:

- This **free safety blitz** is illustrated from a variation of **zero coverage** that is disguised as 2 zone.

- The front is an unbalanced (*under*) variation of the pro 4-3.

- This is an **illusion stunt** that gives the offense the *illusion* that eight defenders are blitzing.

- The free safety is blitzing the strongside A gap. The strong tackle is aligned in a 0 technique and slanting into the weakside A gap. Mike and the strong end are twisting. Mike is responsible for controlling the C gap and *spying* the near back. The strong end is responsible for controlling the B gap. Both Sam and Will are on contained rushes. The weak end is responsible for controlling the C gap and *spying* the near back.

- The defenders filling the gaps are responsible for cutback.

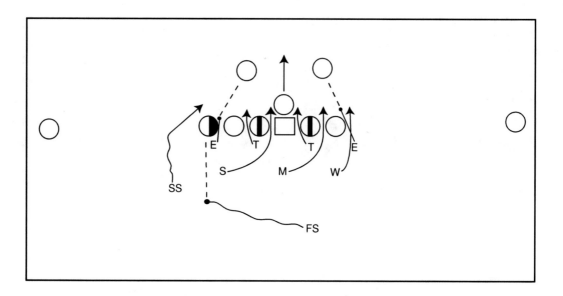

COACHING POINTS:

- This **strong safety blitz** is illustrated from a variation of **zero coverage** that is disguised as 3 sky.

- The front is a balanced variation of the college 4-3.

- This is an **illusion stunt** that gives the offense the *illusion* of an eight-man blitz.

- The strong safety is blitzing the D gap, and is responsible for strongside containment versus both pass and run. Sam is blitzing the strongside A gap, and Mike is blitzing the weakside B gap. Will is blitzing the D gap and is responsible for weakside containment. The strong end is aligned in a 7 technique and is responsible for controlling the C gap. The weak end is aligned in a 7 technique and slanting toward the outside heel of the offensive tackle; he is responsible for controlling the C gap. Both ends are responsible for *spying* the near backs. As the quarterback begins his cadence, the free safety should slowly creep to a position that will enable him to cover the tight end.

- The defenders filling the gaps are responsible for cutback.

STUNT #10

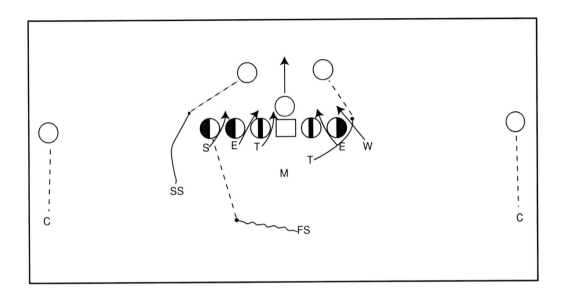

COACHING POINTS:

- This fake **strong safety blitz** is illustrated from a variation of **zero coverage** that is disguised as 3 sky.

- The front is a balanced variation of a pro 4-3 in which the weak tackle is aligned in a flexed 4 technique.

- This is an **illusion stunt** that gives the offense the *illusion* that seven defenders are blitzing.

- The strong safety is faking a blitz through the D gap, and is responsible for strongside run containment. Versus pass, the strong safety will *spy* the near back. Sam, the strong end, and the strong tackle will all stunt to their inside gaps. Mike will *over-read* (i.e., read backfield flow) and check weakside A gap versus runs into this area; he has no strongside gap responsibility. The weak Tackle will twist into the D gap and is responsible for weakside run containment; versus pass, he will *spy* the near back. The weak end will slant into the B gap. Will will blitz toward the outside heel of the offensive tackle and control the C gap. The free safety will creep over and cover the tight end.

- The strong safety and the defenders filling the gaps are responsible for cutback.

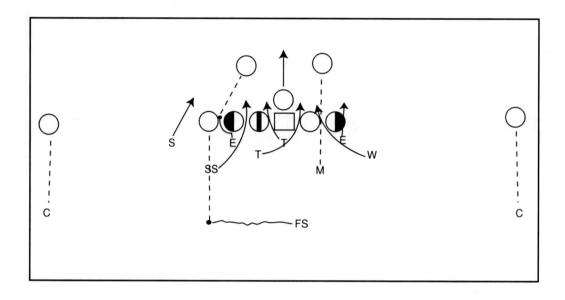

COACHING POINTS:

- This **strong safety blitz** is illustrated from a variation of **zero coverage** that may be interpreted as either 3 sky or cover 1 by the quarterback.

- The front is an unbalanced (*over*) variation of a pro 4-3. The strong tackle is aligned in a flexed 4 technique.

- This is an **illusion stunt** that gives the offense the *illusion* that seven defenders are blitzing.

- The strong safety, who is aligned in a flexed 7 technique, is blitzing the B gap. Sam is on a strong-side containment rush. The strong end is aligned in a 5 technique; he is responsible for controlling the B gap and *spying* the near back. The two tackles are twisting into the A gaps. Will is blitzing into the B gap. The weakside end is aligned in a 5 technique and is responsible for controlling the C gap and containing the quarterback. Mike will not blitz; he will *over-read* and contain all weakside runs. Versus pass, he will cover the near back. The free safety should slowly creep over and cover the tight end.

- Mike and the defenders filling the gaps are responsible for cutback.

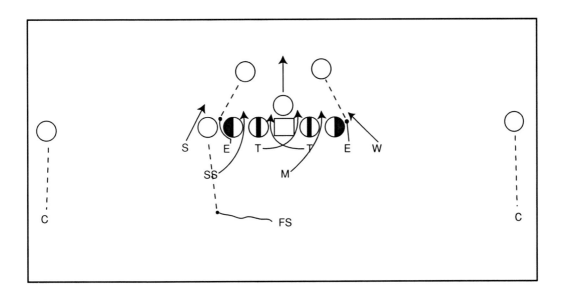

COACHING POINTS:

- This **strong safety blitz** is illustrated from a variation of **zero coverage** that is may be interpreted by the quarterback as either 3 sky or cover 1.

- The front is a balanced variation of the pro 4-3.

- This is an **illusion stunt** that gives the offense the *illusion* of an eight-man blitz.

- The strong safety and Mike are blitzing the B gaps. Both Sam and Will are on a contained rush.

- The two ends are responsible for covering the running backs if a pass develops. Both tackles are twisting into the A gaps. The free safety should slowly creep over and cover the tight end.

- The defenders filling the gaps are responsible for cutback.

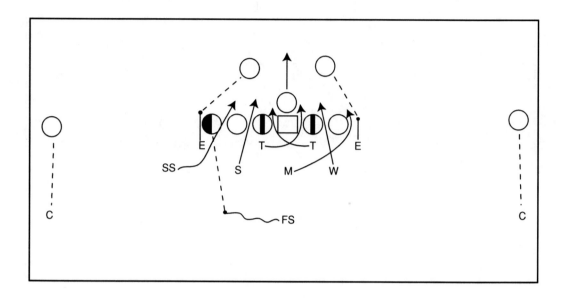

COACHING POINTS:

- This **strong safety blitz** is illustrated from a variation of **zero coverage** that is disguised as 3 sky.

- The front is a balanced variation of the college 4-3.

- This is an **illusion stunt** that gives the offense the *illusion* that eight defenders are blitzing.

- The strong safety will creep inside and blitz the C gap; he is responsible for strongside containment versus pass. Both ends must contain all runs and *spy* the near back versus pass. The two tackles are twisting into the A gaps. Will is blitzing into the B gap, and Mike is blitzing the C Gap. Mike is responsible for controlling the C gap and containing the quarterback. The free safety should slowly creep over and cover the tight end.

- The defenders filling the gaps are responsible for cutback.

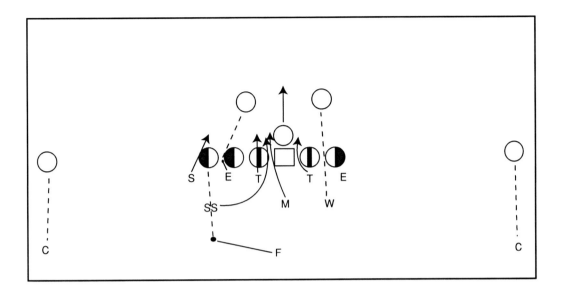

COACHING POINTS:

- This **strong safety blitz** is illustrated from a variation of **zero coverage.**

- The front is a balanced variation of a pro 4-3 in which the strong safety is aligned in a flexed 6 position.

- This is an **illusion stunt** that gives the offense the *illusion* of a seven-man blitz.

- The strong safety will blitz the A gap. Sam will crash from the outside and contain passes and strongside runs. The strong end is responsible for controlling the C gap and *spying* the near back. Mike will blitz through the strongside shoulder of the center. The strong tackle will line up in a 2 technique and control the B gap. The weak tackle will line up in a 2 technique and slant into the A gap. Will will *under-read* runs and cover the near back. The weak end will line up in a 5 technique, control the C gap, and contain the quarterback.

- Will and the defenders filling gaps are responsible for cutback.

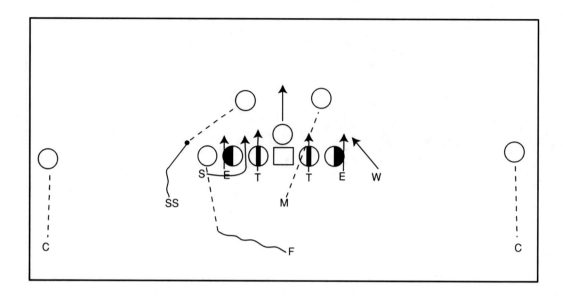

COACHING POINTS:

- This is a **fake strong safety blitz**.

- This stunt is illustrated from a **zero coverage** that is disguised as a 3 sky or cover 1.

- The front is a variation of a pro 4-3.

- The strong safety will creep up and *show blitz*. At the snap of the ball, he will cross the line of scrimmage, contain strongside runs and *spy* the near back. Sam will loop around into the B gap. The strong end will line up in a 5 technique and control the C gap. Both tackles will line up in a 2 techniques and control the B gaps. Mike will *under-read* and control both A gaps. Versus pass, Mike will cover the near back. The weak end will line up in a 5 technique and control the C gap. Will will rush from the outside and contain the quarterback and weakside runs.

- Both Mike and the strong safety are responsible for cutback when flow goes away from them.

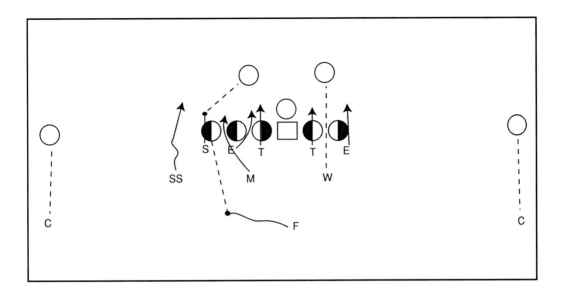

COACHING POINTS:

- This is a **strongside overload stunt**; it's purpose is to overload the strongside with four rushers.

- This stunt is illustrated from a variation of **zero coverage** that is disguised as a cover 1 or 3 sky.

- The front is an unbalanced (*load* or *reduction*) variation of a 4-3.

- The strong safety will creep up and blitz hard on a contain rush. The strong end and Mike will twist.

- The strong tackle will line up in a 1 technique and control the A gap; he must make certain that the center can't reach block him. Sam will line up in a 9 technique, control the C gap, and *spy* the near back. The weak end will line up in a 5 technique, control the C gap, and contain the quarterback. Will will *under-read* run and cover the near back on pass. The free safety must creep over and cover the tight end.

- Both Sam and Will are responsible for cutback when flow goes away from them.

Note: The *under-read* responsibilities and reactions for Will and the weak end from this alignment are as follows: both players read the offensive tackle. If the offensive tackle tries to block him, the Will will scrape into the C gap, and the weak end will squeeze the B gap. If the offensive tackle blocks the weak end, the weak end will control the C gap, and Will will fill the B gap.

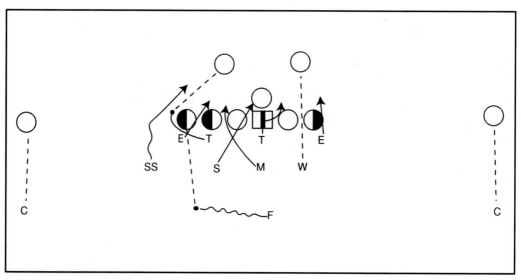

COACHING POINTS:

- This is stunt a **strongside overload;** it's purpose is to overload the strongside with four rushers.

- This stunt is illustrated from a variation of **zero coverage** that is disguised as a 3 sky or cover 1.

- The front is a variation of a pro 4-3, which Hank Stram made popular when he coached at Kansas City. Most coaches still refer to this variation as the *Kansas City stack*.

- The strong safety will creep up and blitz hard on a contain rush. The strong end and tackle will twist. The strongside tackle is responsible for *spying* the near back. Mike will blitz the B gap, and Sam will blitz through the inside shoulder of the offensive guard. Sam can not allow himself to be blocked by the center. The weak tackle will first draw the center's block in an attempt to clear the path for Sam, and then slant into the weakside A gap. The weak end will line up in a 5 technique, control the C gap, and contain the quarterback. Will will *under-read* run and cover the near back on pass. The free safety must creep over and cover the tight end.

- Will and the defenders filling the gaps are responsible for cutback.

NOTE: The best time to use either a strongside or weakside overload stunt is in a passing situation or when a team has an overwhelming tendency to run toward or away from their tight end. The obvious weakness of an overload stunt is a running play away from the overload.

STUNT #18

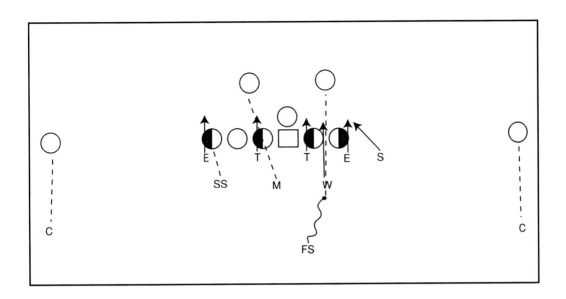

COACHING POINTS:

- This is a **weak side overload stunt**; it's purpose is to overload the weakside with four rushers.

- This stunt is illustrated from a variation of **zero coverage** that is disguised as cover 1.

- The front is an unbalanced variation of a college 4-3 in which the strong safety will line up in flexed 7 technique, and Sam will line up on the weakside.

- The strong end and Sam are on a contain rush. The strong safety will cover the tight end. The strong tackle will line up in a 3 technique and control the B gap. Mike will *over-read* run and cover the near back. The weak tackle will line up in a 1 technique and control the A gap; it is important that he does not allow himself to be blocked by the center. The free safety will creep up and pretend to blitz, but then cover the near back. The weak end will line up in a 5 technique and control the C gap. Will will blitz through the B gap.

- Mike and the free safety are responsible for cutback when flow goes away from them.

STUNT #19

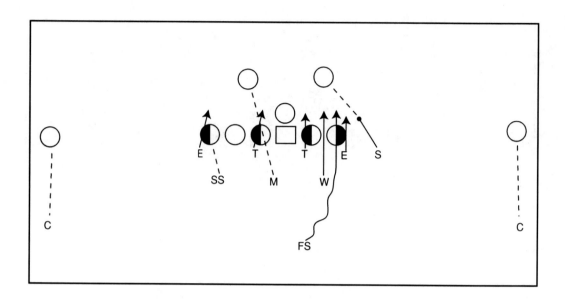

COACHING POINTS:

- This is stunt a **weakside overload;** it's purpose is to overload the weakside with four rushers.

- This stunt is illustrated from a variation of **zero coverage.** It is an excellent pass-situation stunt, but weak against strongside runs.

- The front is variation of a college 4-3 in which the strong safety is lined up in a flexed 7 technique, and Sam is playing on the weakside.

- The free safety will creep up and blitz hard through the nose of the offensive tackle. Will will blitz through the B gap, and the weak end will rush through the outside shoulder of the offensive tackle. The weak end must control the C gap and contain the quarterback. Sam will fake a blitz and *spy* the near back. Against run, Sam has containment. Mike will *over-read* run and cover the near back on pass. The strong tackle will line up in a 3 technique and control the B gap. The strong safety will line up in a flexed 7 technique and cover the tight end. The strong end will line up in a 9 technique, control the D gap, and contain the quarterback.

- Mike and the Sam are responsible for cutback when flow goes away from them.

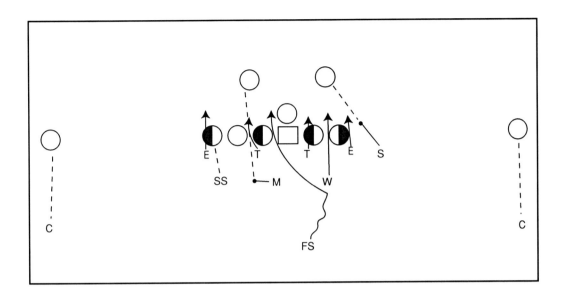

COACHING POINTS:

- This is a stunt that appears to be a **weakside overload,** but ends up exploiting a strongside run audible that a quarterback might call when he suspects a weakside overload blitz. Note: No stunt is necessary to exploit an audible that might be called when a strongside overload is suspected because it is seldom the object of suspicion. Because strongside overloads, especially those involving a strong safety blitz, closely resemble illusion stunts, quarterbacks are seldom suspicious of them.

- This stunt is illustrated from a variation of **zero coverage** that is disguised as cover 1.

- The front is an unbalanced variation of a college 4-3 in which strong safety will line up in a linebacker position, and Sam will line up on the weakside.

- This stunt is identical to Stunt #19, except for the fact that in this stunt, the free safety will blitz the strongside A gap; the strong tackle will slant hard into the B gap, and Mike will shuffle laterally toward the B gap.

- Mike and Sam are responsible for cutback when flow goes away from them.

STUNT #21

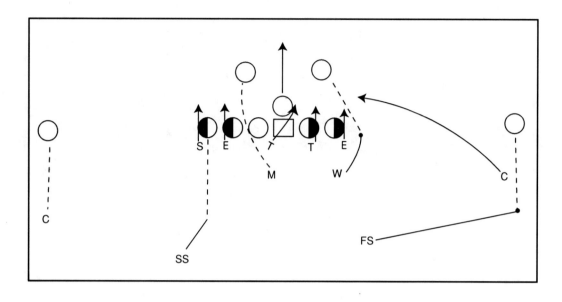

COACHING POINTS:

- This stunt is employed from a variation of **zero coverage** that starts out looking like cover 2. The defense must be careful not to stay in a cover 2 look too long because the free safety must quickly get himself in a position to cover X.

- The front is a balanced variation of a pro 4-3 in which the strong side tackle is aligned in a tilt technique.

- This is **cornerback blitz**. Cornerback blitzes are most effective when the blitzing cornerback is aligned into the boundary, or when the ball is in the middle of the field.

- The weak cornerback is blitzing the D gap; he has only one responsibility and that is to *make a big play*. The weak end will align in a 5 technique, control the C gap, and contain the quarterback. When the ball is snapped, Will will scrape outside, contain all weakside runs and *spy* the near back. The weak tackle will line up in a 3 technique and control the B gap. Sam will align in a 9 technique; he is responsible for containment versus pass and run. The strong end will line up in a 5 technique, control the C gap, and contain the quarterback. The strong tackle will attack the center and attempt to cave the center into the weakside A gap. Mike will *over-read* run and cover the near back versus pass.

- When flow goes away from them, both Will and Mike are responsible for cutback.

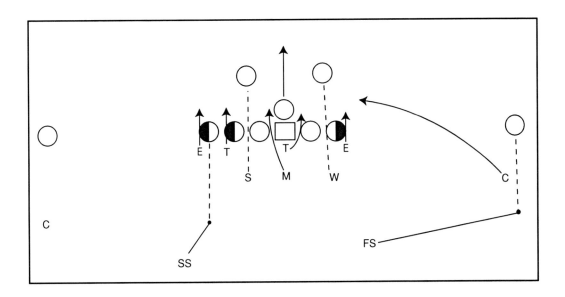

COACHING POINTS:

- This **cornerback blitz** is illustrated from a variation of **zero coverage** that starts out looking like cover 2.

- The front is a (*Kansas City stack*) variation of the pro 4-3

- The weak cornerback is blitzing the D gap and attempting to *make a big play*. Sam and Will are both *under-reading*; they are responsible for covering the near back versus pass. Mike is blitzing, the strongside A gap, and the weak tackle is slanting into the weakside A gap. The strong end is aligned in 9 techniques; he is responsible for containing the quarterback and strongside runs. The strong tackle is lined up in a 5 technique; he must control the C gap. The weak end is aligned in a 5 technique; he must control the C gap and contain the quarterback.

- Will and Mike are responsible for cutback.

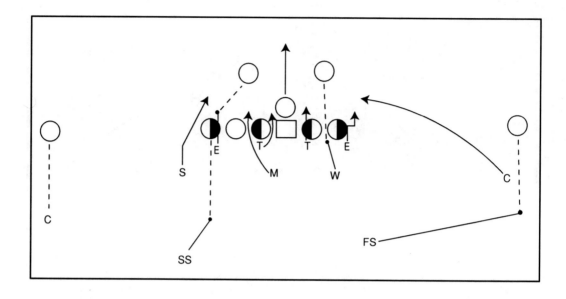

COACHING POINTS:

- This stunt is illustrated from a variation of **zero coverage** that starts out looking like cover 2.

- The front is an unbalanced variation of a college 4-3.

- This is both a **cornerback blitz** and an **illusion stunt** that gives the illusion of an eight-man blitz.

- The weak cornerback is blitzing the D gap and attempting to *make a big play*. Sam is also blitzing the D gap and is responsible for containment versus pass and run. Mike and the strong tackle are twisting. The strong end is aligned in a 7 technique; he must control the C gap and *spy* the near back. Will is faking a blitz into the B gap and *spying* the near back. The weak tackle is lined up in a 1 technique and controlling the A gap. The weak End is aligned in a 5 technique; he is responsible for controlling the C gap and containing the quarterback.

- Will and the defenders filling the gaps are responsible for cutback.

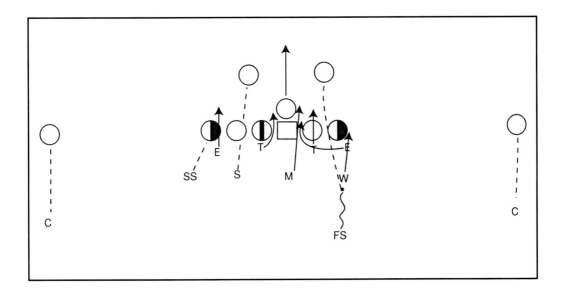

COACHING POINTS:

- This stunt is illustrated from a variation of **zero coverage** in which the free safety fakes a blitz and covers the near back.

- The front is a balanced variation of a college 4-3.

- This is a stunt that rushes six defenders.

- The free safety will creep toward the line and get into a position that will enable him to contain all weakside runs and cover the near back on passes. Will is blitzing through the outside shoulder of the offensive tackle; he must control the C gap and contain the quarterback. The weakside tackle is aligned in a 2 technique; he must control the B gap. At the snap of the ball, the weak end will loop around and blitz the weakside A gap. Mike will blitz through the weakside shoulder of the center. The strong tackle will line up in a 2 technique and slant into the A gap. Sam will line up in a flexed 4 technique, control the B gap, and cover the near back. The strong end will line up in a 7 technique, control the C gap, and contain the quarterback.

- The free safety and Sam are responsible for cutback when flow goes away from them.

STUNT #25

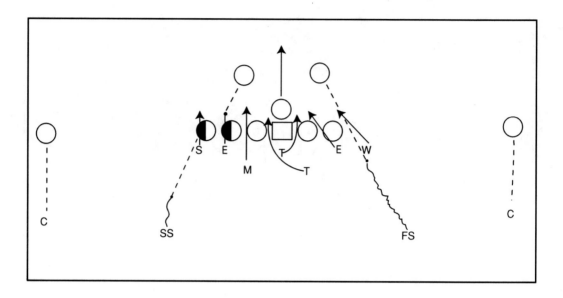

COACHING POINTS:

- This stunt is illustrated from a variation of **zero coverage** in which the free safety *shows blitz* and covers the near back. The stunt starts out looking like either 3 sky or cover 1.

- The front is a balanced (*under*) variation of a pro 4-3 with the weak tackle lined up in a flexed 2 technique.

- This is an **illusion stunt** that gives the illusion of an seven-man blitz.

- Sam will line up in a 9 technique, control the D gap, and contain the quarterback. The strong end will line up in a 5 technique; he is responsible for controlling the C gap and *spying* the near back. Mike will blitz through the outside shoulder of the offensive guard. The strong tackle will line up in a 0 technique and slant into the weakside A gap. The weak tackle will line up in a flexed 2 technique and loop into the strongside A gap. The weak end will line up in a 5 technique and slant into the B gap. Will will control the C gap and contain the quarterback. The free safety will contain all weakside runs and spy the near back.

- The free safety and the defenders filling the gaps are responsible for cutback.

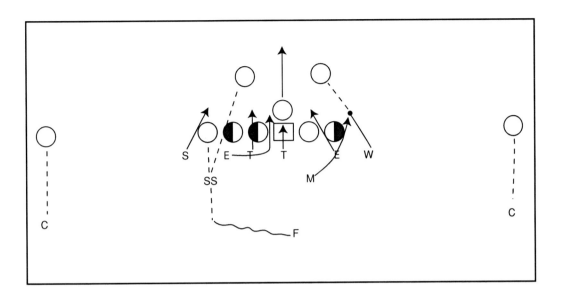

COACHING POINTS:

- This stunt is the last stunt employed from **zero coverage.**

- The front is a balanced (*over*) variation of a pro 4-3.

- This is an **illusion stunt** that gives the illusion of an seven-man blitz.

- Sam will crash from the outside and contain strongside runs and the quarterback. The strong safety will line up in a flexed 7 technique, control the C gap, and cover the near back. At the snap of the ball, the strong end will loop around into the A gap. The strong tackle will line up in a 3 technique and control the B gap. The weak tackle will line up in a 0 technique and control both A gaps. Mike and the weak end will twist. Mike is responsible for containing the quarterback versus pass. Will will fake an outside crash, contain weakside runs and *spy* the near back.

- The free safety and Will are responsible for cutback when flow goes away from them.

CHAPTER 3

COVER 1 STUNTS

Cover 1 is a man-to-man coverage with either the strong safety or the free safety free. This chapter presents the following eight categories of Cover 1 stunts:

- The free safety is free, and three other defenders are locked onto the tight end and the two running backs.

- The free safety is free. Two strongside defenders will *Banjo* the tight end and the strongside halfback, while one weakside defender will cover the weakside halfback.

- The free safety will blitz. The strong safety is free. Two strongside defenders will Banjo the tight end and the strongside halfback, while one weakside defender will cover the weakside halfback.

- The free safety will blitz. The strong safety is free, and three defenders will lock onto the tight end and two running backs.

- The strong cornerback will blitz. The free safety is free. Two strongside defenders will *Banjo* the tight end and the near back, while a weakside defender will cover the weakside halfback.

- The weak cornerback will blitz. The free safety is free. Two strong side defenders will *Banjo* the tight end and the strongside halfback, and one weakside defender will cover the weakside halfback.

- The free safety will fake a blitz and cover the near back. The strong safety is free, and two strongside defenders will *Banjo* the tight end and the strongside halfback.

- The free safety is free. The strong safety will fake a blitz and cover the strongside halfback. Sam will cover the tight end, and a weakside defender will cover the weakside halfback.

The strength of Cover 1 is that there is always a safety who is free, keying the ball, playing center field, and backing up the three other defensive backs and the seven defenders in the box. Another strength of this coverage is that it is a man-to-man coverage and the offense cannot high-low zones of attack in the seams.

Although it is not as risky as zero coverage, Cover 1 does not exert as much pressure on the offense as zero coverage. This weakness can be somewhat offset, however, by incorporating the tactic of *illusion* into its stunt package.

BANJO

Many of the stunts in this chapter include a Banjo technique by two strongside defenders. When Banjo is employed, the two strongside defenders involved will drop to an area and cover either the tight end or the strongside halfback, depending upon which receiver enters their area. The following diagram illustrates how the strong safety and Mike would Banjo two different pass patterns:

Banjo Coverage

Defensive linemen are frequently asked to drop off into an area and cover a receiver when Banjo is employed. I'd briefly like to touch upon the initial steps that a defensive lineman should use when executing a Banjo technique (the same initial steps will be used when defensive linemen are asked to drop off into a zone when a Zone Blitz is called). I believe that a defensive lineman needs to take only two initial steps up the field while reading pass or run. Some coaches believe that they need three initial steps. Perhaps the true answer depends upon the individual player involved. Because of my belief, the following explanation will be based upon the premise of a two-step technique:

- The deeper a defensive lineman lines up when executing the Banjo technique, the easier it will be for him to accomplish his task. It is probably best to start out teaching this technique from a flexed position. As proficiency and confidence are gained, the coach can start moving the defensive lineman closer to the line of scrimmage.

- When involved in Banjo and the lineman is slanting outside, he should step with his outside foot first; therefore, if he is slanting outside (and outside is to his left), he will make his first step with his left foot. His next step will be a crossover step with his right foot. During these two steps, he will read and react to his keys. If he reads pass, he will plant and pivot on his second step. His third step will be with his left foot; this step will open his hips and get him headed in the direction of his drop. If he reads run during his first two steps, he will fill his assigned gap and react.

- When involved in Banjo and the lineman is slanting inside, he will also step with his outside foot first. Therefore, if inside is to the lineman's right, he will make his first step with his left foot. This will be a crossover step. His next step will be with his right foot. During these two steps, he will read and react to his keys. If he reads pass, he will plant and pivot on his second step. This will open his hips to the outside. His third step, which will be with his left foot, will get him headed in the direction of his drop. If he reads run during his first two steps, he will fill his gap and then react. Stunting inside and then dropping outside is extremely difficult (if not impossible) when the defensive lineman takes a flat angle during his first two steps. It is therefore important the lineman gets depth (off the ball) and take his first two steps *toward* the line (rather than parallel to it) when executing this technique.

- When a defensive lineman is off the ball and dropping into coverage from a head-up position (no slant involved), he will step with his outside foot first and then plant and pivot on his second step. When hugging the line of scrimmage, most defensive linemen need to take only one step.

- If a defensive lineman is involved in Banjo coverage and he's also assigned to maintain outside run leverage (protect his outside gap), he will step with his inside foot first. If he's maintaining inside leverage (protecting his inside gap), he'll step with his inside foot first. This will be the only read-step necessary. If the lineman reads pass, he will pivot on his first step and drop into coverage.

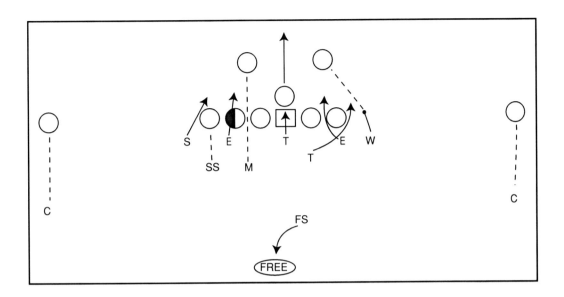

COACHING POINTS:

- This stunt is illustrated from a variation of **Cover 1** in which the free safety is free, and the strong safety is locked onto the tight end.

- The front is an unbalanced (*under*) variation of a pro 4-3. The weak tackle is aligned in flex 4 technique

- This stunt gives the defense a five-man rush versus pass.

- The strong safety will align himself in a flexed 7 technique and cover the tight end man-to-man. Sam is rushing from the outside and containing all passes and runs to his side. The strong end is lined up in a 5 technique and controlling the C gap. Mike is *under-reading*, controlling the B gap and covering the near back. The strong tackle is lined up in a 0 technique and controlling both A gaps. The weak end and weak tackle are twisting; the weak tackle is responsible for containing the quarterback versus pass. Will is assigned to contain all weakside runs and cover the near back on pass.

- Mike and Will are responsible for cutback when flow goes away from them.

STUNT #28

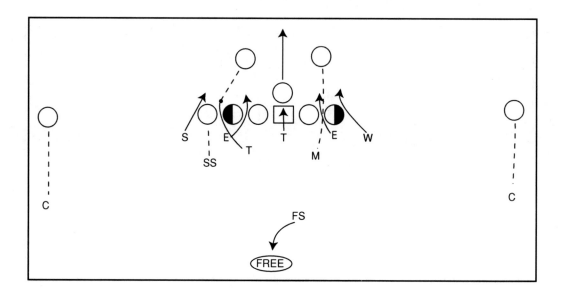

COACHING POINTS:

- This stunt is illustrated from a variation of **Cover 1** in which the free safety is free and the strong safety is locked onto the tight end.

- The front is a balanced (*over*) variation of a pro 4-3. The strongside tackle is aligned in a flexed 4 technique.

- This stunt gives the defense the *illusion* of a six-man rush versus pass.

- The strong safety will align himself in a flexed 7 technique; he is responsible for covering the tight end man-to-man. Sam is rushing from the outside and containing all passes and runs to his side. The strong end and tackle are twisting. The strong tackle is assigned to *spy* the near back versus pass. Will and the weak end are crashing hard to their inside. Mike is *over-reading* and is assigned to contain all weakside runs, and cover the near back on pass.

- Mike and the defenders filling gaps are responsible for cutback.

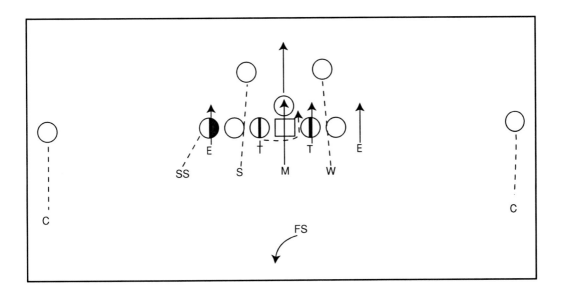

COACHING POINTS:

- This stunt is illustrated from a variation of **Cover 1** in which the free safety is free and the strong safety is locked onto the tight end.

- The front is a variation of a college 4-3.

- The strong safety will align himself in a loose 8 technique and cover the tight end man-to-man. Sam will line up in a flexed 5 technique, scrape into and control the D gap versus strongside runs, and cover the near back versus pass. The strong end will line up in a 7 technique, control the C gap, and contain the quarterback. The strong tackle will line up in a 2 technique, control the B gap versus run, and **delay stunt** through the weakside A gap versus pass. Mike will blitz through the face of the offensive center; he will control both A gaps. The weak tackle will line up in a 2 technique and control the B gap. Will will line up in a flexed 4 technique, control the C gap, and cover the near back. The weak end will line up in a 7 technique, control the D gap, and contain the quarterback.

- Sam and Will are responsible for cutback.

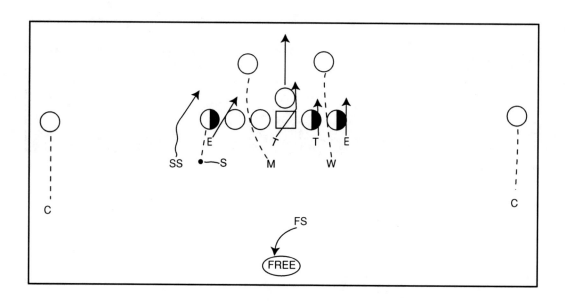

COACHING POINTS:

- This stunt is illustrated from a variation of **Cover 1** in which the free safety is free, the strong safety is blitzing, and Sam is locked onto the tight end. Until the strong safety begins his movement toward the line of scrimmage, the quarterback's pre-snap read will probably be 3 sky.

- The front is a variation of a college 4-3, in which the strongside tackle is aligned in a tilt technique and Mike is lined up behind him.

- The strong safety will blitz the D gap and contain all runs and passes to his side. At the snap of the ball, the strongside end will crash inside and control the C gap, and Sam will shuffle outside and cover the tight end. The strong tackle will attack the center and attempt to cave the center into the weakside A gap. Mike will *over-read* run and cover the near back versus pass. The weak Tackle will line up in a 3 technique and control the B gap. Will will *under-read* run and cover the near back versus pass. The weak end will line up in a 5 technique, control the C gap, and contain the quarterback.

- Mike and Will are responsible for cutback when flow goes away from them.

STUNT #31

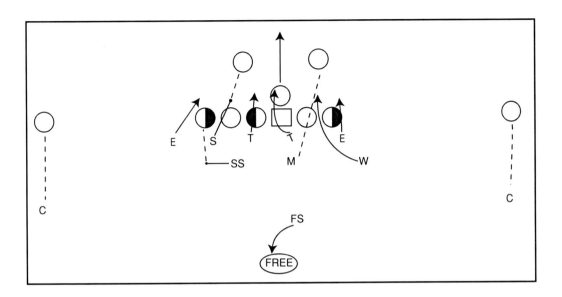

COACHING POINTS:

- This stunt is illustrated from a variation of **Cover 1** in which the free safety is free, and the strong safety is covering the tight end.

- The front is a variation of a college 4-3, in which the strong safety is aligned in a flexed 5 technique, Sam is lined up in a 7, and the strongside end is lined up in an 8. The weak tackle is aligned in a tilt technique, and Mike is lined up behind him.

- At the snap of the ball, Sam will slant into the C gap and *spy* the near back. The strong end will crash and contain all runs and passes to his side. The strong safety will shuffle laterally and cover the tight end. The strong tackle will line up in a 3 technique and control the B gap. The weak tackle will attack the center and attempt to cave the center into the strongside A gap. Mike will *over-read*, fill the A gap on strongside runs, and contain all weakside runs. Versus pass, Mike will cover the near back. Will will blitz the B gap. The weak end will line up in a 5 technique, control the C gap, and contain the quarterback.

- Mike and the defenders filling gaps are responsible for cutback.

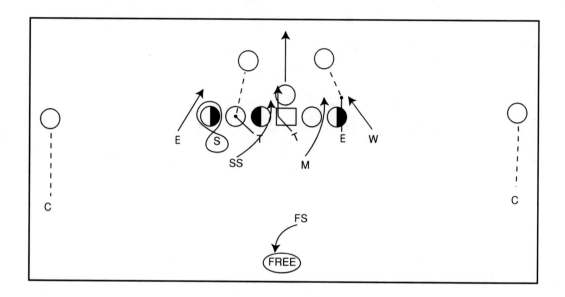

COACHING POINTS:

- This stunt is illustrated from a variation of **Cover 1** in which the free safety is free, the strong safety is blitzing, and Sam is locked onto the tight end.

- The front is a variation of a college 4-3, which is identical to the one illustrated in Stunt #31.

- This stunt is identical to stunt #31 except: the strong safety will blitz the A gap. Sam will cover the tight end. The strong tackle will slant to a 4 technique and *spy* the near back. Mike will blitz the weakside B gap. The weak end will spy the near back, and Will will rush hard from the outside and contain all runs and passes to his side.

- The defenders filling gaps are responsible for cutback.

STUNT #33

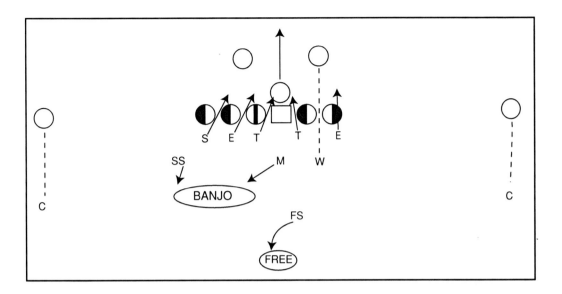

COACHING POINTS:

- This stunt is illustrated from a variation of **Cover 1** in which the free safety is free, and the strong safety and Mike will Banjo the tight end and strongside back versus drop-back action. The alignment of the secondary gives the quarterback a cover 3 pre-snap read.

- The front is a balanced variation of a pro 4-3.

- This stunt gives the defense a five-man rush versus pass.

- The strong safety is responsible for containing all strongside runs. When run action goes away from the strong safety, he is responsible for covering the tight end should the play become a play-action pass. Sam, the strong end, and strong tackle will all slant to their inside gaps. Mike will *over-read* and fill the B gap versus weakside runs; he has no gap responsibility versus strongside runs. Against pass, Mike will drop into Banjo coverage. The weak tackle will line up in a 2 technique and slant into the A gap. Will will *under-read* and cover the near back versus pass. The weak end will line up in a 5 technique, control the C gap, and contain the quarterback.

- Mike and Will are responsible for cutback when flow goes away from them.

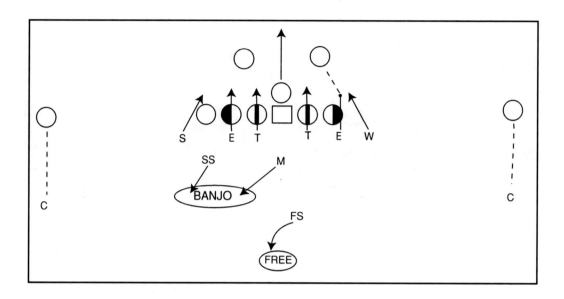

COACHING POINTS:

- This stunt is illustrated from a variation of **Cover 1** in which the free safety is free, and the strong safety and Mike will Banjo drop-back action. When run action goes away from the strong safety, he is responsible for covering the tight end if the play becomes a play-action pass.

- The front is a balanced variation of a pro 4-3.

- This stunt affords the defense excellent containment versus run and a five-man pass rush versus pass.

- The strong safety is lined up in a flexed 6 technique, *over-reading* run, and dropping into Banjo coverage versus pass. Both Sam and Will are charging hard on a contain rush. The ends and Tackles are reading and controlling their outside gaps. Mike is *under-reading* and slow-playing both A gaps versus run. Versus pass, he will drop into Banjo coverage. The weak end is lined up in a 5 technique, controlling the C gap, and *spying* the near back versus pass.

- Mike and the strong safety are responsible for cutback.

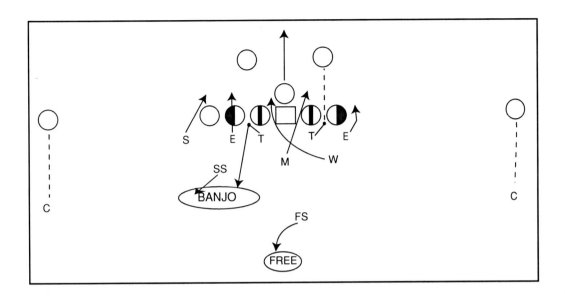

COACHING POINTS:

- This stunt is illustrated from a variation of **Cover 1** in which the free safety is free, and the strong safety and the strongside tackle will Banjo drop-back action. When run action goes away from the strong safety, he is responsible for covering the tight end if the play becomes a play-action pass.

- The front is a balanced variation of a pro 4-3 in which the strong safety has walked up into a flexed 6 position.

- This stunt gives the offensive line and two running backs an immediate *illusion* of a 7-man pass rush.

- The strong safety will *over-read* run and drop into Banjo coverage versus pass. Sam is on a contain rush versus pass and run. The strong end will line up in a 5 technique and control the C gap. The strong tackle will line up in a 2 technique, slant toward the B, control this gap versus run, and Banjo with the strong safety versus pass. The weak tackle will slant outside, control the B gap, and *spy* the near back. The weak end will slant outside; he must contain all passes and runs to his side. Mike and Will are blitzing (with a twist) the A gaps.

- The defenders filling gaps are responsible for cutback versus run.

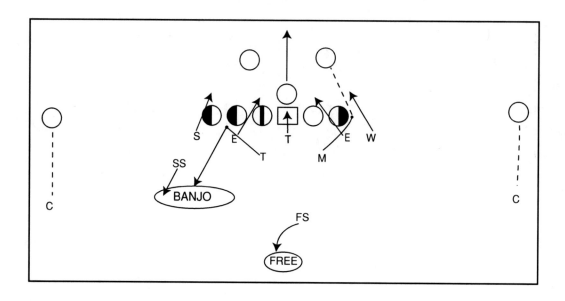

COACHING POINTS:

- This stunt is illustrated from a variation of **Cover 1** in which the free safety is free, and the strong safety and the strongside tackle will Banjo drop-back action. When run action goes away from the strong safety, he is responsible for covering the tight end if the play becomes a play-action pass.

- The front is an unbalanced (*over*) variation of a pro 4-3 in which the strong tackle is playing a flexed 2.

- This stunt gives the offensive line and two running backs an immediate *illusion* of a 7-man pass rush.

- The strong safety is aligned in a loose 8 technique; he is responsible for containing strongside runs and dropping off into Banjo coverage versus pass. Sam is lined up in a 9 technique; he is responsible for controlling the D gap and containing the quarterback. The strong end and tackle are twisting. The strong tackle is responsible for controlling the C gap versus run and dropping into Banjo coverage versus pass. The weak tackle is aligned in a 0 technique and responsible for controlling both A gaps. Mike and the weak end are twisting. Mike is responsible for controlling the C gap versus run and *spying* the near back versus pass. Will is on a contained rush versus pass and run.

- The defenders filling the gaps and the strong safety are responsible for cutback versus run.

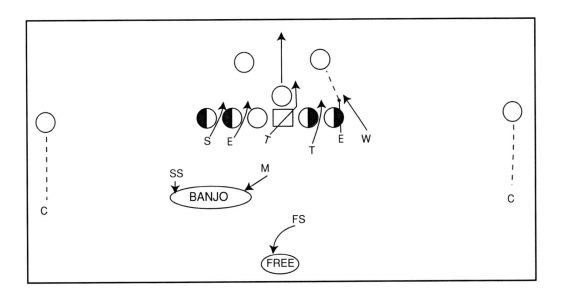

COACHING POINTS:

- This stunt is illustrated from a variation of **Cover 1** in which the free safety is free, and the strong safety and Mike will Banjo versus drop-back action. When run action goes away from the strong safety, he is responsible for covering the tight end if the play becomes a play-action pass.

- The front is a balanced variation of a pro 4-3 in which the strong tackle is playing a tilt technique and the weak tackle is playing a flexed 2. Mike is playing behind the tilted tackle.

- This stunt affords the defense solid inside run support.

- The strong safety is aligned in a loose 8 technique; he is responsible for containing strongside runs and dropping off into Banjo coverage versus pass. Sam and the strong end are crashing inside. Sam is responsible for containing the quarterback against pass. Mike will over-read run and drop into Banjo coverage versus pass. The tilt tackle will attack the center and attempt to cave the center into the weakside A gap. The flexed Tackle will stunt through the outside shoulder of the offensive guard and control the B gap. Will is on a contain rush, and the weakside end will control the C gap versus run and *spy* the near back versus pass.

- Mike and the strong safety are responsible for cutback.

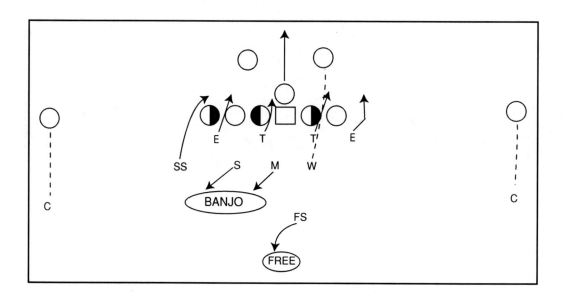

COACHING POINTS:

- This stunt is illustrated from a variation of **Cover 1** in which the free safety is free, and the strong safety will blitz. Sam and Mike will Banjo if they read drop-back action. When run action goes away from the Sam, he is responsible for covering the tight end if the play becomes a play-action pass.

- The front is an unbalanced (*split*) variation of a college 4-3. The front looks vulnerable to a weakside run, but the line slant compensates for this apparent weakness.

- The strong safety is on a contain blitz. The line is slanting to the weakside. The weak end is responsible for containing all passes and runs. Will is responsible for the C gap versus weakside runs and the A gap versus strongside runs. Will must also cover the near back versus pass. Mike will Banjo with Sam versus pass. Mike must also control the B gap versus strongside runs and the A gap versus weakside runs.

- Both Mike and Will are responsible for cutback versus the run.

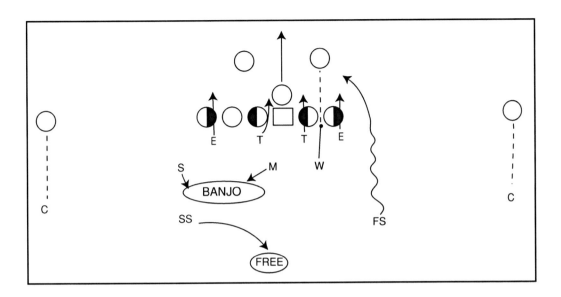

COACHING POINTS:

- This stunt is illustrated from a variation of **Cover 1** that starts out looking like cover 2.

- The stunt features a free safety blitz with the strong safety free. Sam and Mike will Banjo versus drop-back action. When run action goes away from the Sam, he is responsible for covering the tight end if the play becomes a play-action pass.

- The front is an unbalanced variation of a college 4-3.

- This stunt gives the offense the *illusion* of a four-man rush to the weakside.

- The free safety is blitzing outside and containing pass and run. The weak end is aligned in a 5 technique and controlling the C gap. Will is faking a blitz into the B gap and *spying* the near back. The weak tackle is playing a 1 technique and controlling the A gap. Sam is lined up in a loose 8 technique; he must control strongside runs and drop into Banjo coverage versus pass. The strong end is lined up in a 7 technique; he must control the B gap and contain the quarterback. The strong tackle is lined up in a 3 technique and slanting into the A gap. Mike is *over-reading* and quickly filling the B gap versus strongside runs; he has no weakside gap responsibility. Versus pass, Mike will drop into Banjo coverage.

- Mike and Will are responsible for cutback versus the run.

STUNT #40

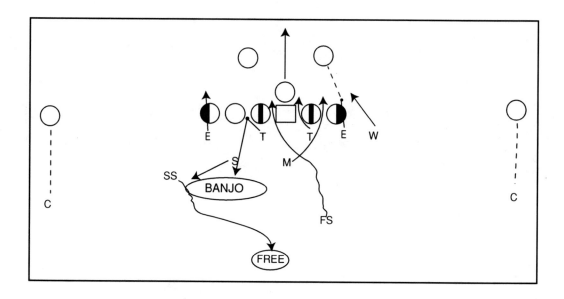

COACHING POINTS:

- This variation of **Cover 1** gives the offense a 3 sky pre-snap read. As the quarterback begins his cadence, the free safety will begin his movement toward the line, and the strong safety will begin moving toward center field. Sam and the strongside tackle will Banjo if they read drop-back action. When run action goes away from the Sam, he is responsible for covering the tight end if the play becomes a play-action pass.

- The front is a balanced variation of a college 4-3

- This stunt gives the offensive line and two running backs an immediate *illusion* of a 7-man pass rush. Although sound versus the run, this is a great stunt to use in a passing situation.

- The strong end is responsible for containing all runs and passes. Sam is responsible the C gap versus the run and Banjo coverage versus the pass. The strong tackle will angle into the B gap and control this gap versus run; versus pass, he will Banjo. The free safety is blitzing the strongside A gap. Mike and the weak tackle are twisting. Will is on a contained rush, and the weak end is controlling the C gap and *spying* the near back.

- The defenders filling gaps are responsible for cutback versus run.

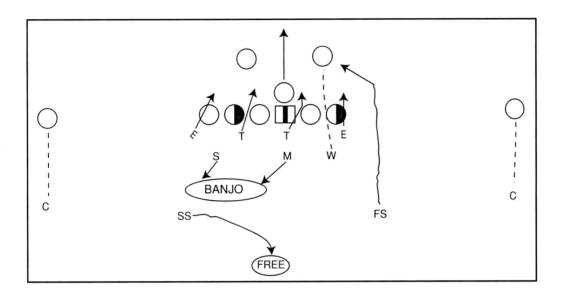

COACHING POINTS:

- This variation of **Cover 1** gives the offense a cover 2 pre-snap read. As the quarterback begins his cadence, the free safety will begin his movement toward the line, and the strong safety will slowly creep toward center field. Sam and Mike will Banjo if they read drop-back action. When run action goes away from the Sam, he is responsible for covering the tight end if the play becomes a play-action pass.

- The front is an unbalanced variation of a pro 4-3 that resembles the *Kansas City stack*.

- The strong end is responsible for containing the quarterback and strongside runs. Sam will line up in a flexed 7 technique; he is responsible for the C gap versus the run and Banjo coverage versus the pass. The strong tackle will line up on the inside shoulder of the offensive tackle and angle into the B gap. Mike will *over-read* run and drop into Banjo coverage versus pass. The weak tackle will line up in a 0 technique and slant into the weakside A gap. The weak end will line up in a 5 technique and control the C gap. Will is responsible for the near back versus pass and *under-reading* run. The free safety is on a controlled containment blitz.

- Sam and Will are responsible for cutback versus run.

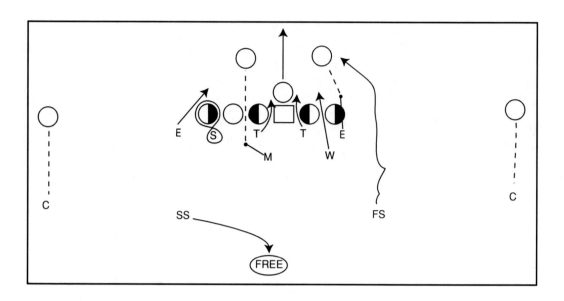

COACHING POINTS:

- This variation of **Cover 1** gives the offense a cover 2 pre-snap read. As the quarterback begins his cadence, the free safety will begin his movement toward the line and the strong safety will slowly creep toward center field. Sam will cover the tight end man-man.

- This is an excellent stunt versus drop-back passes and weakside runs.

- The front is an unbalanced variation of a college 4-3.

- The strong end will line up in an 8 technique and crash inside; he is responsible for containing all runs and passes. The strong tackle will angle into the A gap. Mike will shuffle laterally to the B gap, *over-read* run, and cover the near back versus pass. The weak tackle will line up in a 1 technique and control the A gap. Will will blitz the B gap, and the weak end will control the C gap and *spy* the near back. The free safety will contain the quarterback and weakside runs.

- Mike and the defenders filling gaps are responsible for cutback.

STUNT #43

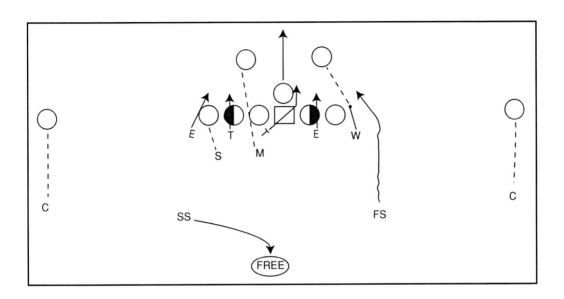

COACHING POINTS:

- This variation of **Cover 1** gives the offense a cover 2 pre-snap read. As the quarterback begins his cadence, the free safety will begin his movement toward the line, and the strong safety will slowly creep toward center field. Sam will cover the tight end man-to-man.

- This is an excellent stunt versus both pass and run. It is extremely effective versus strongside runs.

- The front is an over-shifted variation that has Sam playing a flexed 7 technique. The strong end is playing a tilted 9 technique, and the weak tackle is playing a tilted 0 technique on the strongside. Mike is lined up behind the weak tackle. The weak end is playing a 3 technique, and Will is lined up in a 7 technique.

- The strong end is responsible for containing all passes and strongside runs. The strong tackle must control the C gap. Mike will *over-read* run and cover the near back versus pass. The tilted tackle will attempt to cave the center into the weakside A gap. The weak end will control the B gap, and Will will control the C gap and *spy* the near back. The free safety will blitz and contain all passes and weakside runs.

- Mike and the defenders filling gaps are responsible for cutback.

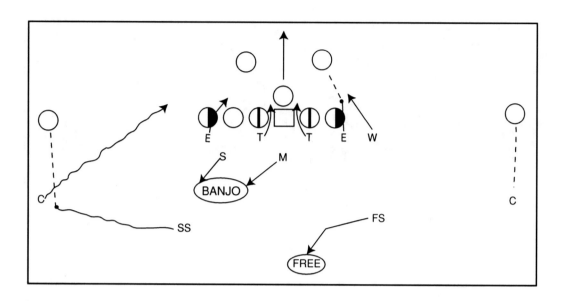

COACHING POINTS:

- This is variation of **Cover 1** that features a **strong cornerback blitz**. The secondary is disguised to give the quarterback a cover 2 pre-snap read. Both Sam and Mike will Banjo when they read drop-back action. When run action goes away from Sam, he must cover the tight end if the play becomes a play-action pass.

- This is an excellent stunt versus both pass and run. It is extremely effective versus strongside runs.

- The front is a balanced variation of a college 4-3.

- The strong cornerback will blitz and attempt to *make a big play*. The strong end will line up in a 7 technique, control the C gap, and contain the quarterback. Sam will line up in a flexed 5 technique and contain all strongside runs by scraping into the D gap. Versus pass, Sam will drop off into Banjo coverage. Both tackles will line up in 2 techniques and pinch into the A gaps. Mike will *over-read* and quickly fill the B gaps versus run and drop into Banjo coverage against pass. The weak end will control the C gap and *spy* the near back. Will will rush hard from the outside and contain the quarterback and weakside runs.

- Sam and Mike are responsible for cutback.

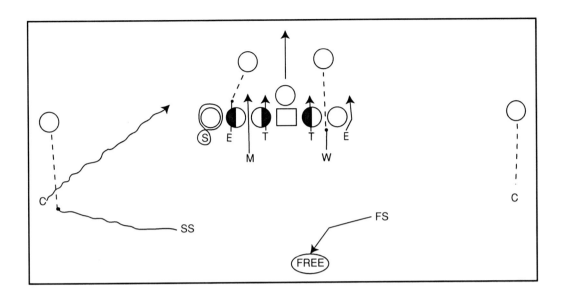

COACHING POINTS:

- This is variation of **Cover 1** that features a **strong cornerback blitz**. The secondary is disguised to give the quarterback a cover 2 pre-snap read. Sam is assigned to cover the tight end man-to-man.

- This is an excellent stunt versus pass and run and strongside runs.

- The front is an unbalanced variation of a pro 4-3.

- The blitzing cornerback must contain all passes and strongside runs. Sam is locked onto the tight end. The strong end will control the C gap and *spy* the near back. Mike will blitz the B gap. Will will fake a blitz into the B gap and spy the near back. The weak end will is assigned to control the C gap and contain the quarterback.

- Will and the defenders filling the gaps are responsible for cutback.

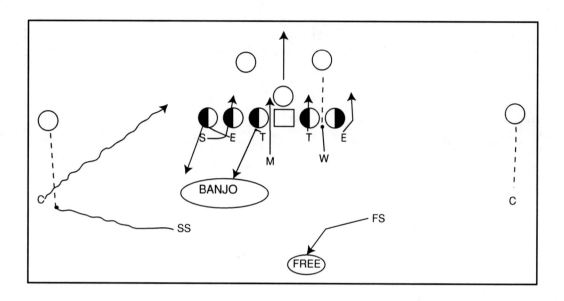

COACHING POINTS:

- This is a variation of **Cover 1** that features a **strong cornerback blitz**. The secondary is disguised to give the quarterback a cover 2 pre-snap read. The strong end and tackle will Banjo drop-back action.

- This is an excellent stunt versus pass and strongside run.

- The front is an unbalanced variation of a pro 4-3.

- The blitzing cornerback must contain all passes and strongside runs. Sam and the strong end will twist. Sam will control the C gap and contain the quarterback. The strong end will control the D gap and drop into Banjo coverage versus pass. The strong tackle will line up in a 3 technique, control the B gap, and drop off into Banjo coverage versus the pass. Mike will blitz the A gap. The weak tackle will line up in a 1 technique and control the A gap. Will will fake a blitz into the B gap and spy the near back. The weak end will is assigned weakside containment.

- The strong end and Will are responsible for cutback.

STUNT #47

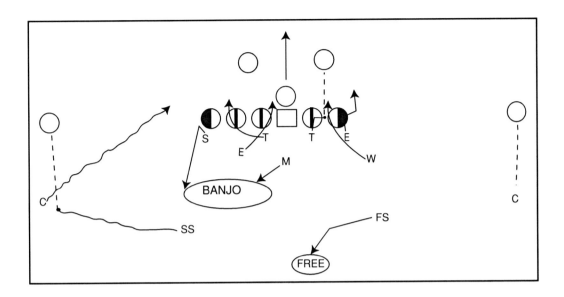

COACHING POINTS:

- This is a variation of **Cover 1** that features a **strong cornerback blitz**. The secondary is disguised to give the quarterback a cover 2 pre-snap read. Sam and Mike will Banjo drop-back action. When run action goes away from Sam, he must cover the tight end if the play becomes a play-action pass.

- This is an excellent stunt versus pass and run.

- The front is a balanced variation of a pro 4-3 with the strongside end flexed in a 4 technique.

- The blitzing cornerback is attempting to *make a big play*. Sam will control the D gap and contain all strongside runs. The strong end and tackle will twist. Mike will *under-read* run and slow play both A gaps; versus pass, he will drop off into Banjo coverage. The weak tackle will control the B gap and *spy* the near back versus pass. Will and the weak end will twist. The weak end is assigned weakside containment.

- Mike is responsible for cutback versus run.

STUNT #48

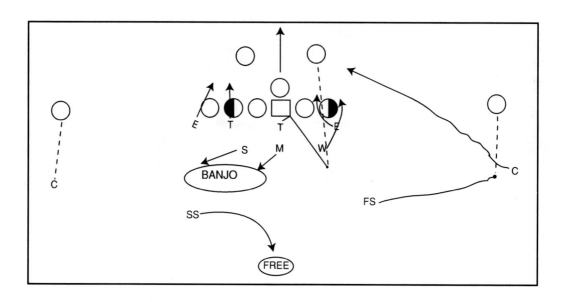

COACHING POINTS:

- This is a variation of **Cover 1** that features a **weak cornerback blitz**. The secondary is disguised to give the quarterback a cover 2 pre-snap read. Sam and Mike will Banjo drop-back action. When run action goes away from Sam, he must cover the tight end if the play becomes a play-action pass.

- This is an excellent stunt versus pass and run.

- The front is an unbalanced (*Kansas City stack*) variation of a pro 4-3 with the strongside end playing a tilt technique.

- The blitzing cornerback is attempting to *make a big play*. The strong end will crash from the outside and contain the quarterback and strongside runs. Sam will *under-read* run and drop off into Banjo coverage versus pass. The strong tackle will line up in a 5 technique and control the C gap. The weak tackle, playing the 0 technique, will control the weakside A gap and drop off and cover the near back versus drop-back pass. Mike will control the strongside A gap versus run and Banjo with Sam versus drop-back pass. Will and the weak end will twist. Will has weakside containment responsibilities.

- Mike and Sam are responsible for cutback.

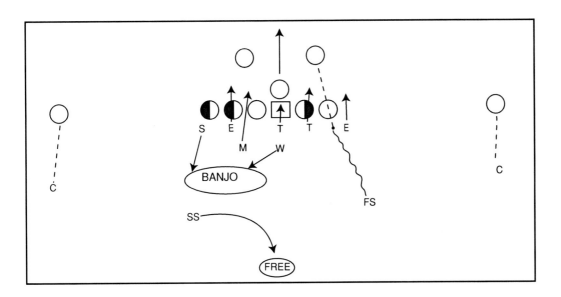

COACHING POINTS:

- This is a variation of **Cover 1** in which the free safety will fake a blitz and cover the near back. The strong safety is free, and Will and Sam will Banjo drop-back action. When run action goes away from Sam, he must cover the tight end if the play becomes a play-action pass.

- This is an excellent stunt versus pass and run.

- The front is an over-shifted variation of the 4-3 that in some ways resembles the *Kansas City stack*.

- Sam will control the D gap and drop into Banjo coverage versus pass. The strong end will control the C gap and contain the quarterback. Mike will blitz the B gap. Will is *over-reading*; he has no specific gap responsibilities versus run. Versus pass, Will will drop into Banjo coverage. The strong tackle, playing the 0 technique, must control both A gaps. The weak tackle has B gap responsibility, and the weak end is responsible for weakside containment. The free safety will control the C gap and cover the near back.

- Will and Sam are responsible for cutback.

STUNT #50

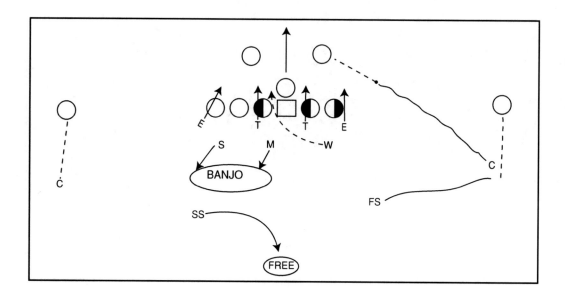

COACHING POINTS:

- This is a variation of **Cover 1** in which the weak cornerback will fake a blitz and cover the near back. The strong safety is free, and Sam and Mike will Banjo drop-back action. When run action goes away from Sam, he must cover the tight end if the play becomes a play-action pass.

- This stunt, which features a **delayed linebacker blitz** versus pass, is excellent versus pass and run.

- The front is an unbalanced variation of a college 4-3; the strong end is playing a tilt technique.

- The strong end will control the D gap and is assigned containment. Sam will *under-read* runs and Banjo drop-back passes. The strong tackle will line up in a 3 technique and control the B gap. Mike will *over-read* runs and Banjo drop-back passes. The weak tackle will line up in a 1 technique and control the A gap. The weak end will line up in a 5 technique, control the C gap, and contain the quarterback. Will will *under-read* runs and **delay blitz** through the strongside A gap versus pass. The weak cornerback will fake the blitz, contain weakside runs, and cover the near back versus pass.

- Sam and Will are responsible for cutback.

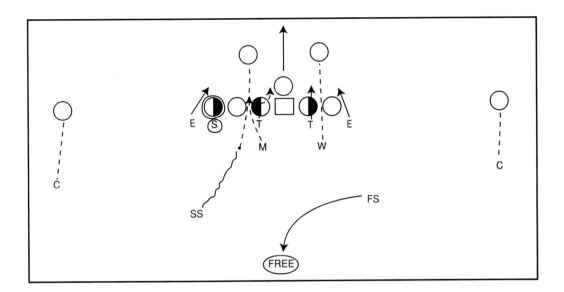

COACHING POINTS:

- This is a variation of **Cover 1** in which the strong safety will fake a blitz and cover the near back. The free safety is free, and Sam is locked on the tight end. The secondary will give the quarterback a cover 2 pre-snap read.

- This stunt features a **delayed blitz**; it is excellent versus pass and run.

- The front is an unbalanced variation of a college 4-3, with the weak end playing a tilt technique.

- The strong end will line up in an 8 technique, crash from the outside, and contain the quarterback and strongside runs. The strong tackle is responsible for the B gap. Mike will *over-read* run and slow play the A gaps. Versus pass, Mike and the strong tackle will **delay blitz.** The strong tackle will delay rush into the A gap, and Mike will delay blitz into the B gap. The weak tackle will control the B gap. The weak end will control the C gap and contain the quarterback. The Will will *over-read*, contain weakside runs, and cover the near back on pass

- Will and the strong safety are responsible for cutback versus run.

STUNT #52

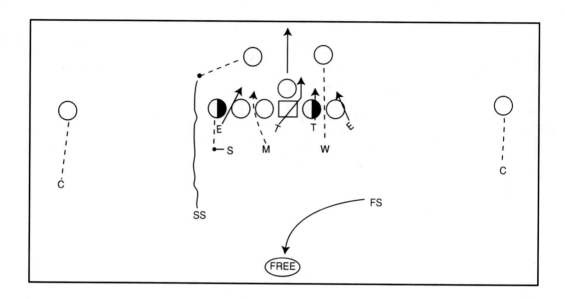

COACHING POINTS:

- This is a variation of **Cover 1** in which the strong safety will fake a blitz and cover the near back. The free safety is free, and Sam is locked on the tight end. The secondary will give the quarterback a cover 2 pre-snap read.

- This stunt features a **delayed linebacker blitz**; it is excellent versus pass and run.

- The front is variation of a college 4-3 in which the strong tackle and the weak end are playing tilt techniques.

- The strong safety will fake an outside blitz, contain strongside runs, and cover the near back versus pass. The strong end will slant inside, control the C gap, and contain pass. Sam will shuffle laterally and cover the tight end. Mike will *over-read* run and quickly fill the B gaps; versus pass, he will **delay blitz** the strongside B gap. The tilt tackle will attempt to cave the center into the weakside A gap. The weak tackle will control the B gap. The weak end will control the C gap and contain the quarterback. The Will will contain weakside runs and cover the near back on pass

- Will and the strong safety are responsible for cutback versus run.

CHAPTER 4

COVER 2 STUNTS

This chapter presents stunts for both **Cover 2 man** and **Cover 2 zone**. The purpose of **Cover 2 zone** is to disrupt the timing of the passing game and get good run support from the cornerbacks. When Sam, Mike and Will are assigned to drop off into coverage, their keys and responsibilities for **Cover 2 zone** are as follows:

5 UNDER   2-DEEP ZONE

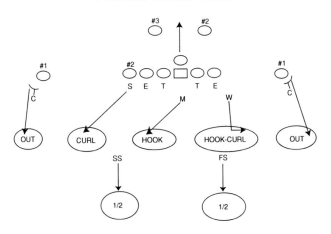

4 UNDER 2-DEEP ZONE

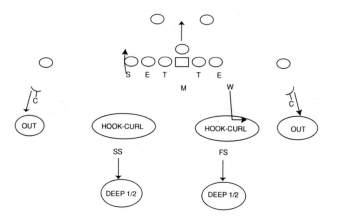

Cornerbacks: Funnel #1 on to the inside. Maintain outside leverage on this receiver and use your hands to disrupt his route. If #1 releases inside, shuffle inside with him for a few steps and then sink deep and wide, keying #2 and #3 (the tight end and strongside halfback). If #1 releases outside, try to maintain outside leverage. If you lose outside leverage, try to ride #1 out of bounds. If both #1 and #2 run vertical routes, run deep with #1. When #1 releases inside and #2 or #3 releases into the flats, be prepared to rally up, but don't let #1 sneak back behind you. If #2 or #3 tries to turn an out route upfield (out and up), collision and run with him.

Sam: Drop immediately to the curl zone. Key #1 (the flanker). Expect that #1 will run a slant, post, or curl. If #1 runs a vertical route, key #2 and #3 (the tight end and strongside halfback). If you're not threatened by either of these receivers, sink to a depth of 18 yards, keeping your head on a swivel.

Mike: Open up and drop 12-15 yards deep into the hook zone. Key #2 (the tight end). If #2 runs a vertical route, stay in the hook and collision him. If #2 tries to cross your face, collision him and look for another receiver to threaten your zone. Be on the alert for a receiver crossing behind you.

Will: Drop hook-curl. Open up and drop 12-15 yards deep into the hook zone. Key #2 (the weakside halfback). If #2 runs a vertical route, stay in the hook and collision him. If #2 releases into the flats, sprint to the curl and look for #1 to run a curl or a post. If #2 runs inside and across your face, look for another receiver (especially the tight end) to run a crossing route into your zone.

Safeties: You have deep 1/2. Stay as deep as the deepest receiver. Read #1and #2. Work toward the receiver who goes deep. If both receivers go deep, move outside of #2 so that you will be able to break to #1.

NOTE: Normally, **Cover 2 zone** is a five-under, two-deep coverage. Some of the stunts covered in this chapter illustrate a four-under, two-deep variation of **Cover 2 zone**. The purpose of this variation is to get an extra pass rusher by blitzing a strongside defender. If, for example, we were to blitz Sam and drop only four defenders into the under coverage, we would have to adjust the coverage by assigning Mike to a *hook-curl* drop (see illustration #2).

When **Cover 2 man** is used, the two cornerbacks will jam the wide receivers and play a bump-and-run technique. Instead of jamming and funneling the wide receivers inside (as they did with **Cover 2 zones**), the cornerbacks will jam and funnel the wide receivers to the outside.

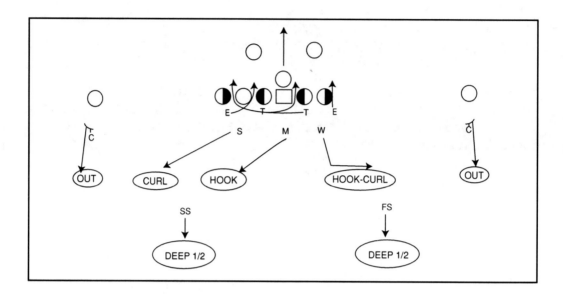

COACHING POINTS:

- This is a **5 under, 2 deep** variation of **Cover 2.**

- The front is variation of a college 4-3.

- This stunt is a **delayed line twist** that occurs only when the defensive line reads pass. The strong end will line up in a 7 technique and control the C gap; versus pass, he will immediately twist into the B gap. Sam will line up in a flexed 5 and scrape into the D gap versus strongside run; versus pass, Sam will drop CURL. The strong tackle will line up in a 3 and control the B gap; versus pass, he will immediately twist into the weakside A gap. Mike will *over-read* run and drop HOOK versus pass. The weak tackle will line up in a 1 technique and control the A gap; versus pass, he will twist into the strongside C gap and contain the passer. The Will will *over-read* and drop HOOK-CURL versus pass. The weak end is responsible for containment.

- Will and the Sam are responsible for cutback versus run.

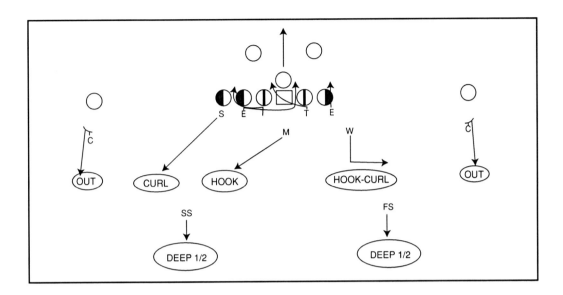

COACHING POINTS:

- This is a **5 under, 2 deep** variation of **Cover 2.**

- The front is variation of a pro 4-3.

- This is a **delayed line twist** that occurs only when the defensive line reads pass. The strong end will line up in a 5 technique and control the C gap; versus pass, he will immediately twist into the weakside A gap. Sam will line up in a 9 technique and control the D gap versus strongside runs; versus pass, Sam will drop CURL. The strong tackle will line up in a 2 technique and control both the A and B gaps; versus pass, he will immediately twist into the strongside C gap and contain the passer. Mike will *over-read* run and drop HOOK versus pass. The weak tackle will line up in a 2 technique and control both the A and B gaps; versus pass, he will attack the center and work into the strongside A gap. The weak end will line up in a 5 technique, control the C gap, and contain the quarterback. The Will will contain weakside runs and drop HOOK-CURL versus pass.

- Will and the Sam are responsible for cutback versus run.

STUNT #55

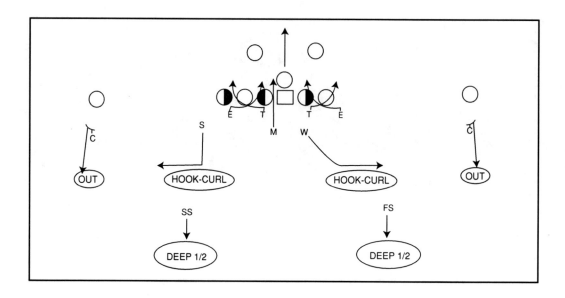

COACHING POINTS:

- This is a **4 under, 2 deep** variation of **Cover 2.**

- The front is an unbalanced (*split*) variation of a college 4-3.

- Along with the linebacker blitz, this is a **delayed line twist** that occurs only when the defensive line reads pass. The strong end will line up in a 7 technique and control the C gap; versus pass, he will immediately twist into the strongside B gap. Sam will line up in a flexed 8 technique and control the D gap; versus pass, he will drop HOOK-CURL. The strong tackle will line up in a 3 technique and control the B gap; versus pass, he will twist into the strongside C gap and contain the passer. Mike will blitz the A gap. The weak tackle will line up in a 3 technique and control the B gap; versus pass, he will twist into the C gap and contain the quarterback. The Will will *over-read* run and drop HOOK-CURL versus pass. The weak end is responsible for weakside run containment; versus pass, he will twist into the weakside A gap.

- Will and the Sam are responsible for cutback.

STUNT #56

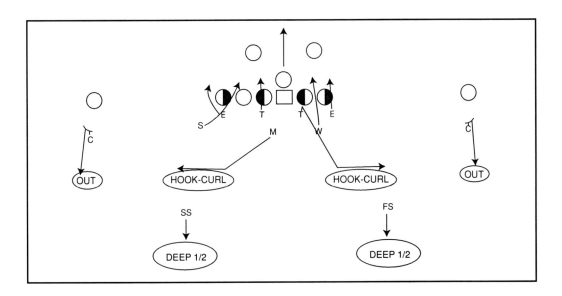

COACHING POINTS:

- This is a **4 under, 2 deep** variation of **Cover 2.**

- The front is an unbalanced variation of a college 4-3.

- This is a **zone blitz**. The strong end will line up in a 7 technique and slant into the D gap; he must contain the quarterback and strongside runs. Sam will line up in a flexed 8 technique and blitz the C gap. The strong tackle will line up in a 3 technique and control the B gap. Mike will *over-read* run and drop HOOK-CURL versus pass. The weak tackle will line up in a 1 technique and control the A gap; versus pass, he will drop HOOK-CURL. The Will will blitz the B gap. The weak end is responsible for weakside containment.

- Mike is responsible for cutback versus run.

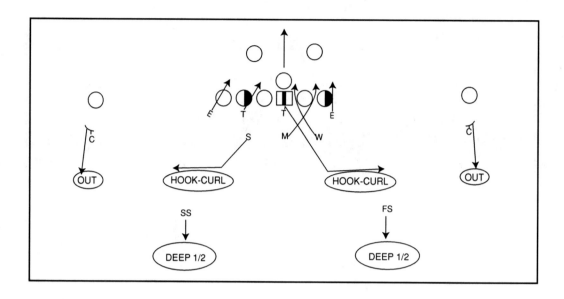

COACHING POINTS:

- This is a **4 under, 2 deep** variation of **Cover 2.**

- The front is an unbalanced (*Kansas City stack*) variation of the 4-3 with the strong end playing a tilt technique.

- This is a **zone blitz**. The strong end will line up in a tilted 9 technique and control the D gap; he must contain the quarterback and strongside runs. Sam will line up in a flexed 4 technique, *under-read* runs, and drop HOOK-CURL versus pass. The strong tackle will slant into and control the B gap. Mike will blitz the weakside B gap. The weak tackle will line up in a 0 technique and control the strongside A gap; versus pass, he will drop HOOK-CURL. The Will will blitz the A gap. The weak end is responsible for weakside containment.

- Sam and the defenders filling the gaps are responsible for cutback versus run.

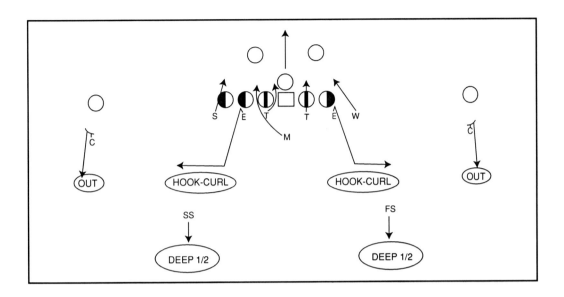

COACHING POINTS:

- This is a **4 under, 2 deep** variation of **Cover 2.**

- The front is a balanced variation of a pro 4-3.

- This is a **zone blitz**. The strong end will line up in a 5 technique and control the C gap; versus pass, he must drop HOOK-CURL. Sam will line up in a 9 technique, rush hard from the outside, and contain the quarterback and strongside runs. The strong tackle will line up in a 2 technique and slant into the A gap. Mike will blitz the B gap. The weak tackle will line up in a 2 technique and control both the weakside A and B gaps. The Will will blitz hard from the outside and contain the quarterback and weakside runs. The weak end is responsible for controlling the C gap versus run and dropping HOOK-CURL versus pass.

- The defenders filling the gaps are responsible for cutback versus run.

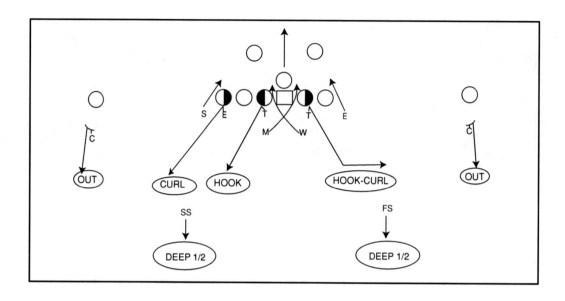

COACHING POINTS:

- This is a **5 under, 2 deep** variation of **Cover 2.**

- The front is an unbalanced (*split*) variation of the 4-3.

- This is a **zone blitz**. The strong end will line up in a 7 technique and control the C gap; versus pass, he must drop CURL. Sam will line up in an 8 technique, rush hard from the outside, and contain the quarterback and strongside runs. The strong tackle will line up in a 3 technique and control the B gap. Versus pass, the strong tackle will drop HOOK. Mike will blitz the weakside A gap. The weak tackle will line up in a 3 technique and control the B gap; versus pass, he will drop HOOK-CURL. The Will will blitz the strongside A gap. The weak end will line up in a 7 technique and contain the quarterback and weakside runs.

- The defenders filling the gaps are responsible for cutback versus run.

STUNT #60

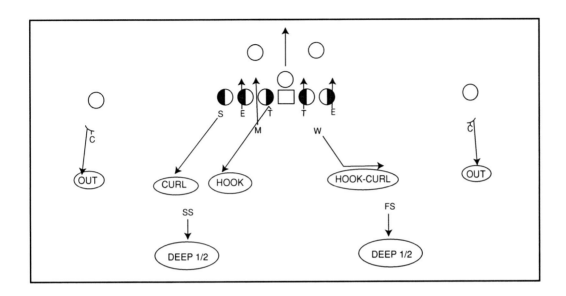

COACHING POINTS:

- This is a **5 under, 2 deep** variation of **Cover 2.**

- The front is an unbalanced (*reduction or load*) variation of a pro 4-3.

- This is a **zone blitz**. The strong end will line up in a 5 technique and control the C gap; versus pass, he must contain the quarterback. Sam will line up in a 9 technique, control the D gap, and drop CURL versus pass. The strong tackle will line up in a 1 technique and control the A gap; versus pass, he will drop HOOK. Mike will blitz the B gap. The weak tackle will line up in a 1 technique and control the A gap. Will's assignment is to *under-read* run and drop HOOK-CURL versus pass. The weak end will line up in a 5 technique, control the C gap, and contain the quarterback on pass.

- Will and Sam are responsible for cutback versus run.

STUNT #61

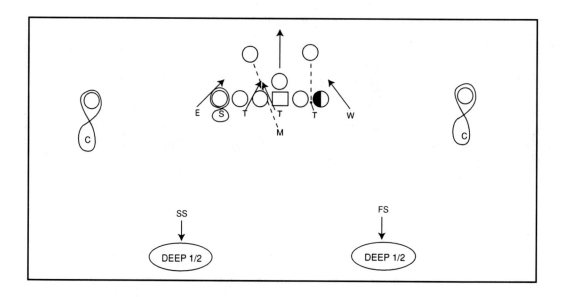

COACHING POINTS:

- This is variation of **Cover 2 man.**

- The front is a variation of a pro 4-3 that resembles the *Kansas City stack.*

- The strong end will line up in an 8 technique and contain run and pass. Sam will line up in a 7 technique and guard the tight end man-to-man. The strong tackle will line up shading the inside of the offensive tackle; he will slant into the B gap. The weak tackle will line up in a 0 technique and stunt into the strongside A gap. Mike will *over-read* run and cover the near back. The weak end will line up shading the inside of the offensive tackle; he will control the B gap and *spy* the near back. Will is on a contain rush.

- Mike is responsible for cutback.

STUNT #62

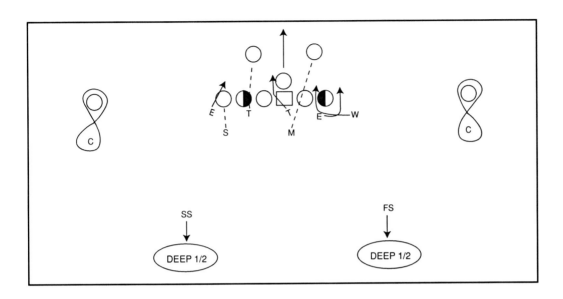

COACHING POINTS:

- This is a variation of **Cover 2 man.**

- The front is variation of a college 4-3 in which the strong end and weak tackle are both lined up in a tilt position.

- The strong end will line up in a tilted 9 technique and contain the quarterback and strongside runs. Sam will line up in a flexed 7 technique and guard the tight end man-to-man. The strong tackle will line up on the inside shoulder of the offensive tackle; he will control the B gap and spy the near back. The weak tackle will line up in a tilted 0 technique, attack the center, and control both A gaps. Mike will line up behind the tilted tackle *over-read* run and cover the near back versus pass. Will and the weak end will twist. The weak end must contain the quarterback and weakside runs.

- The defenders filling the gaps are responsible for cutback.

STUNT #63

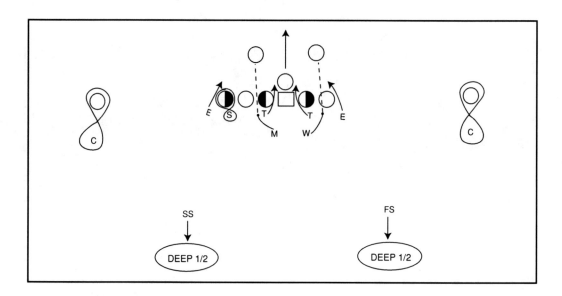

COACHING POINTS:

- This is a variation of **Cover 2 man.**

- The front is variation of a college 4-3 that gives the offense a *split* look.

- The strong end will line up in a tilted 8 technique, rush hard from the outside, and contain the quarterback and strongside runs. Sam will line up in a 7 technique and guard the tight end man-to-man. Both tackles will line up in 3 techniques and slant into the A gaps. Will and Mike will fake blitzes into the B gaps, control these gaps versus run, and *spy* the near back versus pass. The weak end must contain the quarterback and weakside runs.

- The defenders filling the gaps are responsible for cutback versus run.

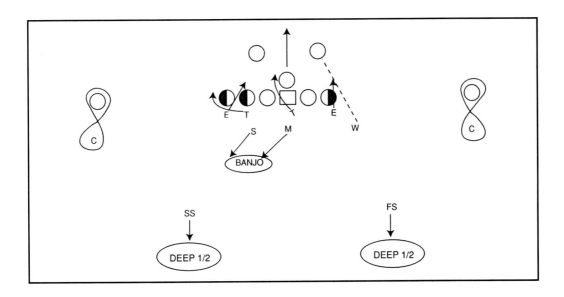

COACHING POINTS:

- This is a variation of **Cover 2 man** in which Sam and Mike will **Banjo** the tight end and strongside halfback.

- The front is variation of a pro 4-3 that resembles the *Kansas City stack*.

- The strong end will line up in a 9 technique, and the strong tackle will line up in a 5; they will twist at the snap of the ball. The strong tackle is responsible for containing the quarterback and strongside runs. Sam will control the B gap versus run and Banjo versus pass. The weak tackle will line up in a tilt and control both A gaps. Mike will line up behind the tilted tackle, *over-read* runs, and Banjo drop-back passes. The weak end will line up in a 5 technique, control the C gap, and contain the quarterback when he reads pass. The Will will line up in in a flexed 7 technique, contain weakside runs, and check the B gap versus strongside runs. Versus pass, Will will cover the near back.

- Sam is responsible for checking both the tight end and cutback when flow goes away from him. Will is responsible for cutback when flow goes away from him.

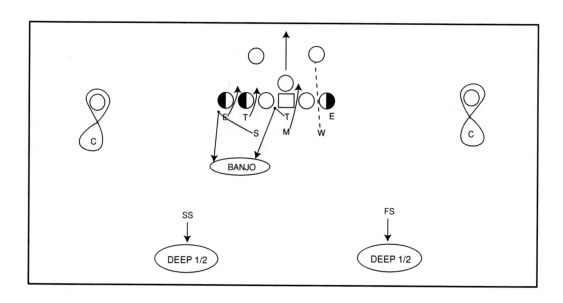

COACHING POINTS:

- This is a variation of **Cover 2 man** in which Sam and the weak tackle will **Banjo** drop-back passes. When flow goes away from Sam, he must cover the tight end if a play-action pass develops.

- The front is variation of a pro 4-3 that resembles the *Kansas City stack*.

- The strong end and strong tackle will slant into their inside gaps when the ball is snapped. The strong end is responsible for containing pass. Sam will stunt to the outside shoulder of the tight end. Sam will contain strongside runs and drop off into Banjo coverage versus pass. The weak tackle will slant into the A gap and drop off into Banjo coverage versus pass. Mike will blitz the A gap. The Will will *under-read* and cover the near back if pass develops. The weak end is responsible for containment.

- Will, Sam, and the defenders filling the gaps are responsible for cutback.

STUNT #66

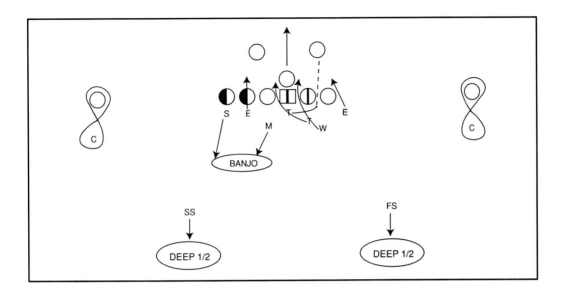

COACHING POINTS:

- This is a variation of **Cover 2 man** in which Sam and the weak tackle will **Banjo** drop-back passes. When flow goes away from Sam, he must cover the tight end if the play becomes a play-action pass.

- The front is an (*under*) variation of the 4-3 in which the weak tackle is flexed.

- Sam will line up in a 9 technique, contain strongside runs, and Banjo drop-back passes. The strong end is assigned to control the C gap and contain passes. Mike is responsible for the B gap versus strongside runs and Banjo coverage versus pass. The strong and weak tackles will twist. The weak tackle will twist into the strongside A gap. The strong tackle will twist into the weakside B gap and *spy* the near back. The weak end is responsible for containment, and the Will will blitz into the A gap.

- Sam and the defenders filling the gaps are responsible for cutback.

CHAPTER 5

COVER 3 STUNTS

This chapter presents stunts for the following variations of **Cover 3**:

- Strong sky

- Weak sky

- Strong cloud

- Weak cloud

- Cover 3 solid with a free safety blitz

- Cover 3 solid with a strong safety blitz

If Sam, Mike, and Will were asked to drop off onto coverage and strong sky was called (refer to Diagram 5-1), the keys and responsibilities for this coverage would be as follows:

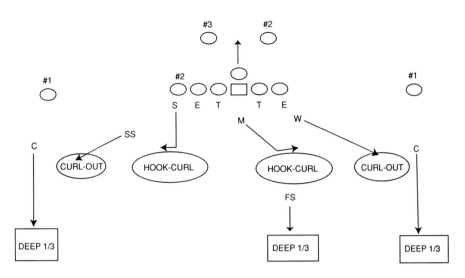

STRONG SKY

Diagram 5-1

- Sam: Drop hook-curl. Drop to a depth of 12-15 yards into the strong hook zone. Key #2 (the tight end). If #2 runs a vertical route, stay in the hook and collision him. If #2 releases into the flats, sprint to the curl and look for #1 to run a curl or a post. If #2 runs inside and across your face, try to collision him, and then look for another receiver to run a crossing route into your zone.

- Mike: Drop hook-curl. Open up and drop to a depth of 12-15 yards into the weak hook zone. Key #2 (the weakside halfback). If #2 runs a vertical route, stay in the hook and collision him. If #2 releases into the flats, sprint to the curl and look for #1 to run a curl or a post. If #2 runs inside and across your face, try to collision him and then look for another receiver to run a crossing route into your zone.

- Strong safety: Drop curl-out. Open up and drop to a depth of 10-12 yards. Your aiming point is three yards inside of where #1 (the flanker) lined up. Key #1. If #1 runs an out, try to get into the throwing lane and get a piece of the ball. If #1 runs a curl or a post, stay inside of his pattern and check #2 (the tight end). If #2 runs an out, you must release from #1's curl or post when #2 crosses your face. If #1 runs a vertical route, sink and check #2 and #3 (the strongside halfback).

- Will: Drop curl-out. Open up and drop to a depth of 10-12 yards. Your aiming point is three yards inside of where #1 (the split end) lined up. Key #1. If #1 runs an out, try to get into the throwing lane and get a piece of the ball. If #1 runs a curl or a post, stay inside of his pattern and check #2 (the weakside halfback). If #2 runs an out, you must release from #1's curl or post when #2 crosses your face. If #1 runs a vertical route, sink and check #2.

- Cornerbacks: You have deep outside 1/3. See both #1 and #2 as you backpedal. Stay as deep as the deepest receiver in your zone. If #1 runs a short or intermediate route, look for #2 to threaten you deep. If #2 also runs a short or intermediate route, control the speed of your back-pedal so that you can break on the ball. If #1 runs a vertical route, maintain a cushion of 3-4 yards. If #1 runs a post, stay on his outside hip and maintain a sufficient cushion.

- Safety: You have deep 1/3. You must drop midway between the two cornerbacks, stay as deep as the deepest receiver, and play center field. Key #2's release. If it is vertical, you must get into a position to cover it. If #2's route is short, check the split end and flanker for the post.

When a cloud variation of **Cover 3** is used, such as strong cloud (refer to Diagram 5-2), the strong cornerback will employ a similar technique to the one he uses in cover 2 zone. The only difference is that the cornerback will remain in the out zone and not have to worry about a receiver sneaking behind him because the strong safety is responsible for the deep one-third.

STRONG SKY

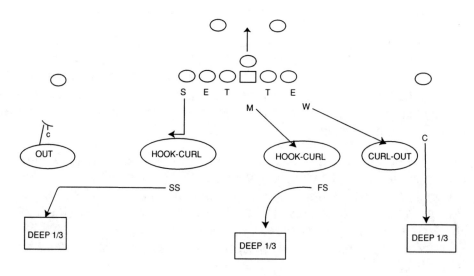

Diagram 5-2

STUNT #67

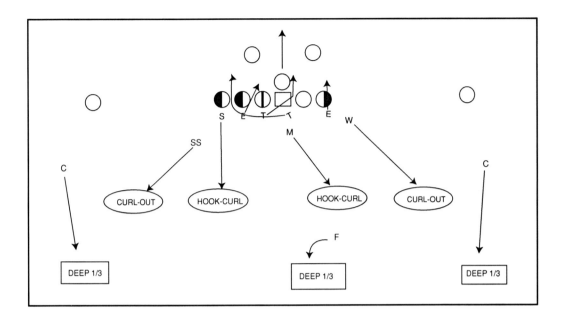

COACHING POINTS:

- This is a **strong sky** variation of **Cover 3.**

- The front is a balanced variation of a pro 4-3 in which the weak tackle is tilted.

- This stunt will occur at the snap of the ball. Sam will line up in a 9 technique, contain strongside runs, and drop HOOK-CURL versus pass. The strong end will slant into the B gap. The strong tackle will slant into the center and try to cave the center into the weakside A gap. The tilted Tackle will loop around into the strongside C gap; he must contain the quarterback if a pass develops. Mike will stack behind the tilted tackle, fill the weakside A gap versus run, and drop HOOK-CURL against pass. The weak end will control the C gap and contain the quarterback on pass. Will is assigned to contain all weakside runs and drop CURL-OUT versus pass.

- Sam and Will are responsible for cutback.

STUNT #68

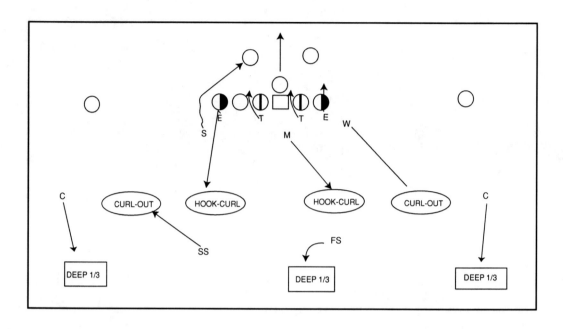

COACHING POINTS:

- This is a **strong sky** variation of **Cover 3**. The secondary is aligned in a cover 2 disguise.

- The front is a balanced variation of a pro 4-3 in which the strong end and Sam have widened.

- This stunt employs **zone blitz** principles. Sam will line up in a flexed 8 technique, slowly creep up as the quarterback calls signals, and stunt hard on a contain rush. The strong end will line up in a 7 technique, control the C gap, and drop HOOK-CURL versus pass. The two tackles will line up in 2 techniques and slant toward the strongside. Mike will over-read, slow play strongside runs, and fill the B gap versus weakside runs. Against pass, Mike will drop HOOK-CURL. Will's assignment is to contain all weakside runs and drop CURL-OUT versus pass.

- The strong safety and Will are responsible for cutback.

STUNT #69

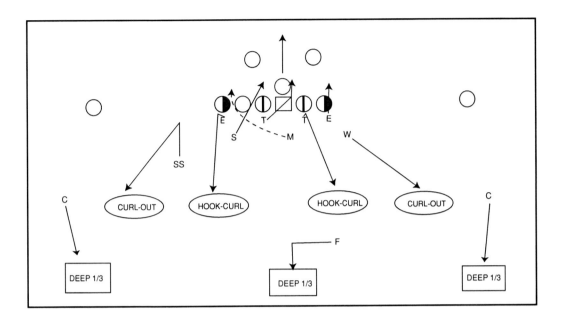

COACHING POINTS:

- This is a **strong sky** variation of **Cover 3**.

- The front is a balanced variation of a college 4-3.

- This is a **zone blitz** that gives the quarterback a pre-snap read that a strong safety blitz is in progress. As the quarterback gets under center, the strong safety will start moving toward the line of scrimmage and give the look that he's blitzing. The strong safety is responsible for containing strongside runs and dropping CURL-OUT versus pass. To enhance the look, the free safety will creep toward the tight end as the strong safety moves up. The strong end will line up in a 7 technique, control the C gap, and drop HOOK-CURL versus pass. Sam will blitz the B gap. The strong tackle will line up in a 2 technique and slant directly at the center; he will try to cave the center into the weakside A gap. Mike will over-read runs and delay blitz through the outside shoulder of the offensive tackle if pass develops. Against pass, Mike is responsible for strongside containment of the quarterback. The weak tackle will control the B gap and drop HOOK-CURL versus pass. The weak end will control the C gap and contain the quarterback against pass. Will's assignment is to contain all weakside runs and drop CURL-OUT versus pass.

- The strong safety and Will are responsible for cutback.

STUNT #70

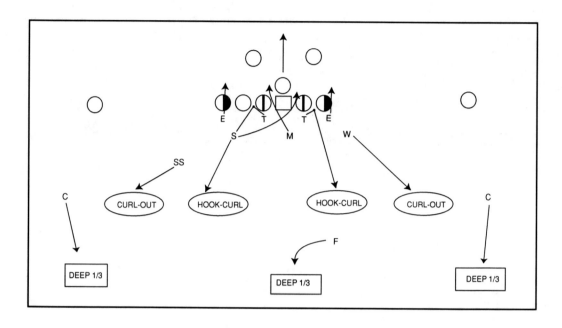

COACHING POINTS:

- This is a **strong sky** variation of **Cover 3**.

- The front is a balanced variation of a college 4-3.

- This is a **zone blitz**. The strong safety will play a loose 8 technique and is responsible for containing strongside runs and dropping CURL-OUT versus pass. The strong end will line up in a 7 technique, control the C gap, and contain the quarterback if pass develops. Both tackles will line up in 2 techniques, slant into the B gaps, and drop HOOK-CURL versus pass. Sam will blitz the weakside A gap, and Mike will blitz the strongside A gap. The weak end will control the C gap and contain the quarterback against pass. Will's assignment is to contain all weakside runs and drop CURL-OUT versus pass.

- The strong safety and Will are responsible for cutback.

- This is an excellent call in a passing situation.

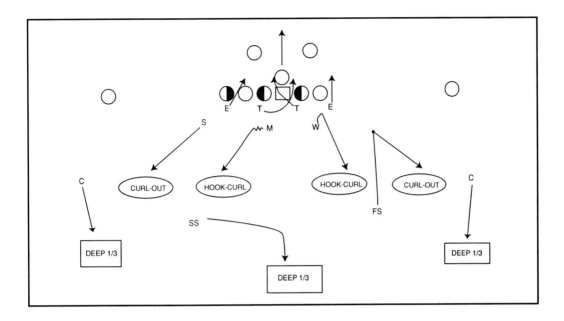

COACHING POINTS:

- This is a **weak sky** variation of **Cover 3**.

- The front is an unbalanced variation of a college 4-3.

- The quarterback is given a pre-snap read that a free safety blitz is in progress. As the quarterback gets under center, the free safety will start moving toward the line of scrimmage and give the look that he's blitzing. The free safety is responsible for containing weakside runs and dropping CURL-OUT versus pass. Sam will line up in a loose 8 technique, contain strongside runs, and drop CURL-OUT against pass. The strong end will line up in a 7 technique, slant into the C gap, and contain the quarterback if pass develops. Mike will over-read runs and drop HOOK-CURL against pass. The strong tackle will loop into the weakside A gap. The weak tackle will line up in a 1 technique and crash into the center, attempting to cave the center into the strongside A gap. The Will will move toward the line and threaten to blitz through the inside shoulder of the offensive tackle. If pass develops, Will is assigned to drop HOOK-CURL. The weak end will control the C gap and contain the quarterback against pass.

- Sam and Will are responsible for cutback.

STUNT #72

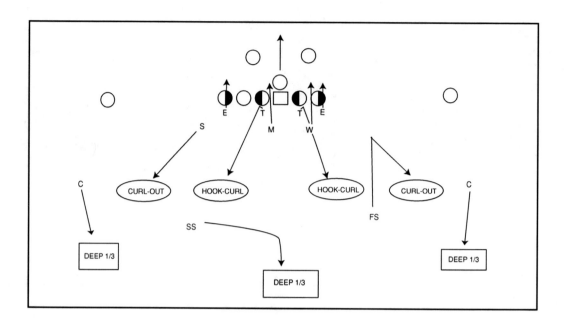

COACHING POINTS:

- This is a **weak sky** variation of **Cover 3**.

- The front is an unbalanced variation of a college 4-3.

- This is a **zone blitz** that gives the quarterback a pre-snap read that a free safety blitz is in progress. Prior to the snap, the free safety will start moving toward the line of scrimmage and give the look that he's blitzing. The free safety is responsible for containing weakside runs and dropping CURL-OUT versus pass. Sam will line up in a loose 8 technique, contain strongside runs, and drop CURL-OUT against pass. The strong end will line up in a 7 technique, control the C gap, and contain the quarterback if pass develops. Mike will blitz the A gap. The strong tackle will line up in a 3 technique, control the B gap, and drop HOOK-CURL versus pass. The weak tackle will line up in a 1 technique, control the A gap, and drop HOOK-CURL versus pass. The Will will blitz the B gap. The weak end is responsible for controlling the C gap and containing the quarterback if a pass develops.

- Sam and the free safety are responsible for cutback.

STUNT #73

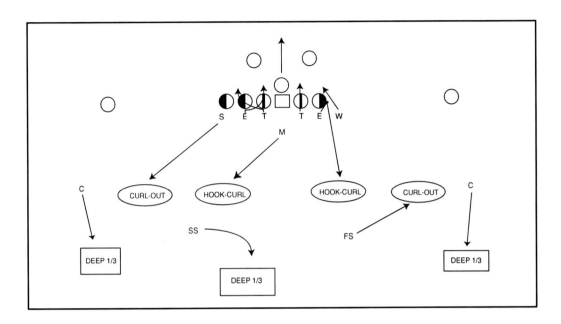

COACHING POINTS:

- This is a **weak sky** variation of **Cover 3**. The secondary is disguised in a cover 2 look.

- The front is a balanced variation of a pro 4-3.

- This stunt incorporates **zone blitz** principles. Sam will line up in a 9 technique, control the D gap, and drop CURL-OUT against pass. The strong end will line up in a 5 technique, control the C gap, and **delay stunt** through the outside shoulder of the offensive tackle (loop around) if pass develops. The strong tackle will line up in a 2 technique, control the B gap, and **delay stunt** (attack the offensive tackle's inside shoulder and then work for outside containment) if pass develops. Mike will over-read runs and drop HOOK-CURL versus run. The weak end will line up in a 5 technique, control the C gap, and drop HOOK-CURL versus pass. Will is on a containment blitz.

- Sam is responsible for cutback.

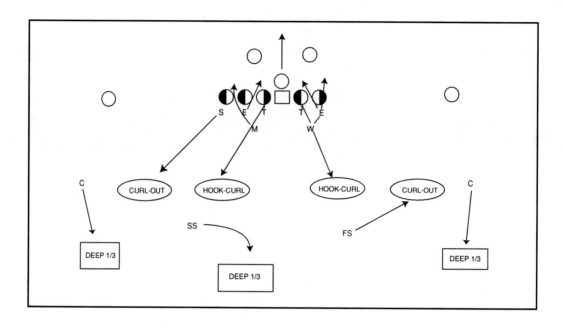

COACHING POINTS:

- This is a **weak sky** variation of **Cover 3**. The secondary is disguised in a cover 2 look.

- The front is an unbalanced (load or reduction) variation of a pro 4-3.

- This stunt is a **zone blitz**. Sam will line up in a 9 technique, control the D gap, and drop CURL-OUT against pass. Both ends will line up in 5 techniques and slant into the B gaps. Will and Mike and will blitz into the C gaps and contain the quarterback if a pass develops. Both tackles will line up in 1 techniques, control the A gaps, and drop HOOK-CURL versus pass.

- The defenders filling the gaps are responsible for cutback.

STUNT #75

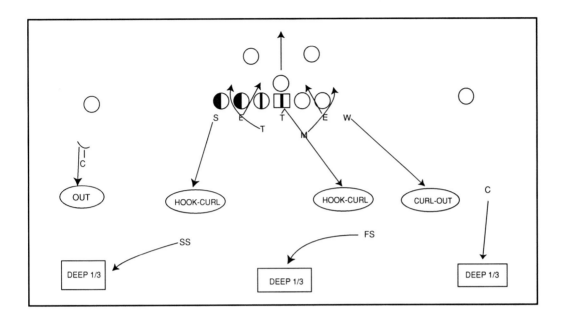

COACHING POINTS:

- This is a **strong cloud** variation of **Cover 3**. The secondary is disguised in a cover 2 look.

- The front is a balanced (over) variation of a pro 4-3 with the strong tackle flexed.

- This stunt incorporates **zone blitz** principles. Sam will line up in a 9 technique, control the D gap, and drop HOOK-CURL against pass. Both ends will line up in 5 techniques and slant into the B gaps. The strong tackle will twist into the C gap and contain the quarterback versus pass. The weak tackle will line up in a 0 technique, control both A gaps, and drop HOOK-CURL against pass. Mike and Will blitz into the C gap and contain the quarterback if a pass develops. The Will will contain weakside runs and drop CURL-OUT versus pass.

- Will and Sam are responsible for cutback.

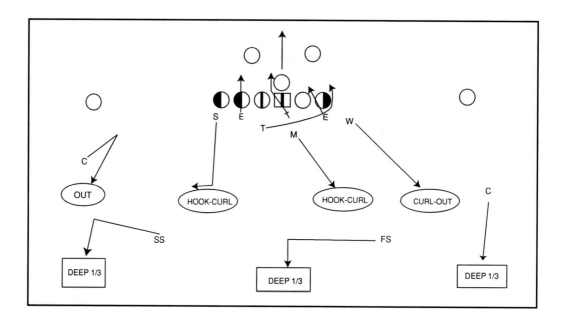

COACHING POINTS:

- This is a **strong cloud** variation of **Cover 3**. The secondary initially gives the quarterback a cover 2 look, but as the quarterback begins his cadence, the secondary will then begin faking a strong cornerback blitz.

- The front is a balanced (over) variation of a pro 4-3, with the strong tackle aligned in a flex, and the weak tackle aligned in a tilt.

- The strong cornerback will pretend to fake a blitz, and the strong safety will pretend to move to a position that will enable him to cover the flanker. At the snap of the ball, however, the strong cornerback will drop CURL-OUT, and the strong safety will cover the deep third. Sam will line up in a 9 technique, control the D gap, and drop HOOK-CURL against pass. Both ends will line up in 5 techniques. The strong end will control the C gap and contain the quarterback versus pass. The weak end will slant into the B gap. The strong tackle will loop around into the weakside C gap and contain the quarterback versus pass. The weak tackle will attack the center and attempt to crush the center into the strongside A gap. Mike will over-read run and drop HOOK-CURL versus pass. The Will will contain weakside runs and drop CURL-OUT against pass.

- Will and Sam are responsible for cutback.

STUNT #77

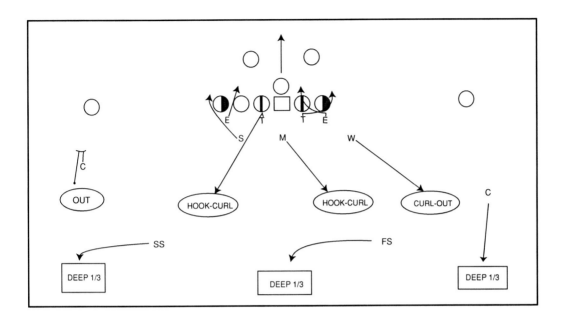

COACHING POINTS:

- This is a **strong cloud** variation of **Cover 3**. The secondary is disguised in a cover 2 look.

- The front is a balanced variation of a college 4-3.

- At the snap of the ball, Sam will stunt to the outside shoulder of the tight end, control the D gap, and contain the quarterback versus pass. The strong end will line up in a 7 technique and slant into the C gap. Both tackles will line up in a 2 technique and control the B gaps. Versus pass, the strong tackle will drop HOOK-Curl, and the weak tackle will **delay stunt** with the weak end. In executing this **delay stunt**, the weak tackle will attack the inside shoulder of the offensive tackle and then work toward containment, and the weak end will loop around and attack the outside shoulder of the offensive guard. Mike will under-read run and drop HOOK-CURL versus pass. The Will will contain weakside runs and drop CURL-OUT against pass.

- Will and the Sam are responsible for cutback.

STUNT #78

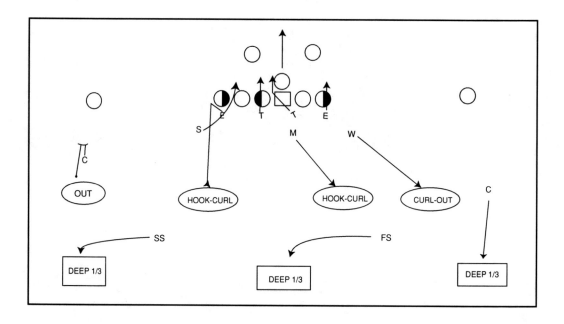

COACHING POINTS:

- This is a **strong cloud** variation of **Cover 3**. The secondary is disguised in a cover 2 look.

- The front is a balanced variation of a pro 4-3 in which the strongside defenders have widened, and the weak tackle is aligned in a tilt.

- This stunt incorporates **zone blitz** principles. At the snap of the ball, Sam and the strong end will twist. Sam will stunt through the outside shoulder of the offensive tackle, control the C gap, and contain the quarterback versus pass. The strong end will slant to the outside shoulder of the tight end, control the D gap, and drop HOOK-CURL against pass. The strong tackle will line up in a 3 technique and control the B gap. The tilted tackle will attempt to crush the center into the strongside A gap. Mike will line up behind the tilted tackle, over-read run, and drop HOOK-CURL versus pass. The weak end will line up in a 5, control the C gap, and contain the quarterback. The Will will contain weakside runs and drop CURL-OUT versus pass.

- Will and the strong end are responsible for cutback.

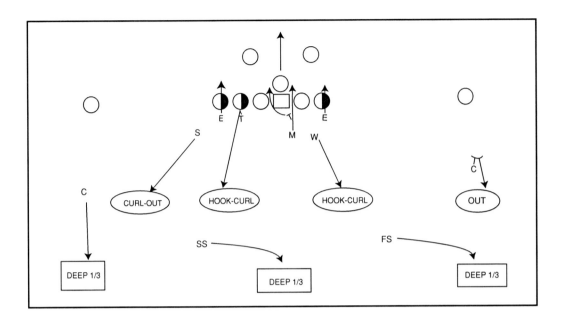

COACHING POINTS:

- This is a **weak cloud** variation of **Cover 3**. The secondary is disguised in a cover 2 look.

- The front is a balanced variation of a pro 4-3 in which the strongside defenders have widened, and the weak tackle is aligned in a tilt.

- This stunt incorporates **zone blitz** principles. Sam will line up in a loose 8, control the D gap, and drop CURL-OUT versus pass. The strong end will line up in a 7 technique, control the C gap, and contain the quarterback. The strong tackle will line up on the inside shoulder of the offensive tackle, control the B gap, and drop HOOK-CURL versus pass. The tilted tackle will slant across the center's face into the strongside A gap. Mike will line up behind the tilted tackle and blitz the weakside A gap. The weak end will line up in a 5 technique, control the C gap, and contain the quarterback. The Will will under-read runs and drop CURL-OUT versus pass.

- Will and Sam are responsible for cutback.

STUNT #80

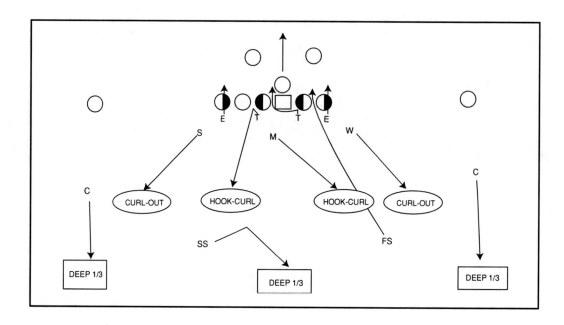

COACHING POINTS:

- This is a variation of **Cover 3 solid** that employs a free safety blitz.

- The front is an unbalanced variation of a college 4-3.

- This stunt incorporates **zone blitz** principles. As the quarterback approaches the center, the free safety will move toward the line of scrimmage and blitz the B gap. Sam will line up in a loose 8, control the D gap, and drop CURL-OUT versus pass. The strong end will line up in a 7 technique, control the C gap, and contain the quarterback. The strong tackle will line up in a 3 technique, control the B gap, and drop HOOK-CURL versus pass. Mike will over-read run and drop HOOK-CURL versus pass. The weak tackle will line up in a 2 technique, control the weakside A gap versus run, but rush through the strongside A gap if he reads pass. The weak end will line up in a 5 technique, control the C gap, and contain the quarterback. The Will will contain weakside runs and drop CURL-OUT versus pass.

- Will and Sam are responsible for cutback.

STUNT #81

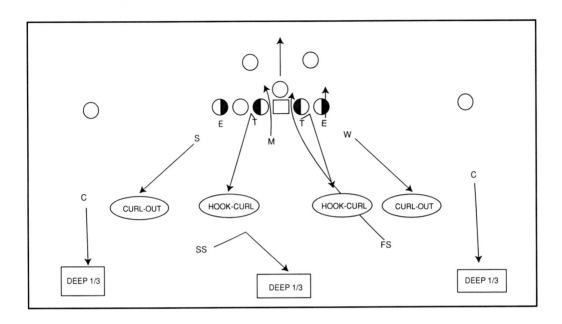

COACHING POINTS:

- This is a variation of **Cover 3 solid** that employs a free safety blitz.

- The front is a balanced variation of a pro 4-3 in which the strongside defenders have widened.

- This stunt incorporates **zone blitz** principles. As the quarterback approaches the center, the free safety will move toward the line of scrimmage and blitz the A gap. Sam will line up in a loose 8, control the D gap, and drop CURL-OUT versus pass. The strong end will line up in a 7 technique, control the C gap, and contain the quarterback. Both tackles will line up in 3 techniques, control the B gaps, and drop HOOK-CURL versus pass. The weak end will line up in a 5 technique, control the C gap, and contain the quarterback. The Will will contain weakside runs and drop CURL-OUT versus pass.

- Will and Sam are responsible for cutback.

STUNT #82

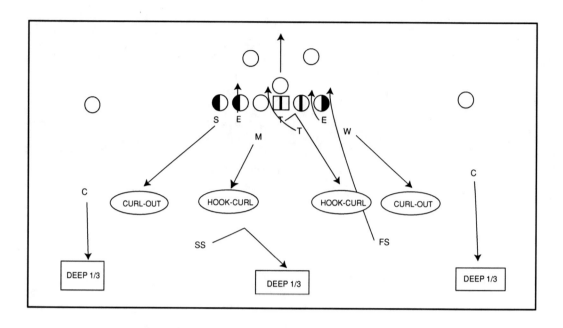

COACHING POINTS:

- This is a variation of **Cover 3 solid** that employs a free safety blitz.

- The front is a balanced (under) variation of a pro 4-3 in which the weakside tackle is flexed.

- This stunt incorporates **zone blitz** principles. As the quarterback approaches the center, the free safety will move toward the line of scrimmage and blitz through the outside shoulder of the offensive tackle, control the C gap, and contain the quarterback. Sam will line up in a 9 technique, control the D gap, and drop CURL-OUT versus pass. The strong end will line up in a 5 technique, control the C gap, and contain the quarterback. The strong tackle will line up in a 0 technique, slant into the weak A gap when the ball is snapped, and drop HOOK-CURL versus pass. The weak tackle will stunt into the strongside A gap. The weak end will line up in a 5 technique and slant into the B gap. The Will will contain weakside runs and drop CURL-OUT versus pass.

- Will and Sam are responsible for cutback.

STUNT #83

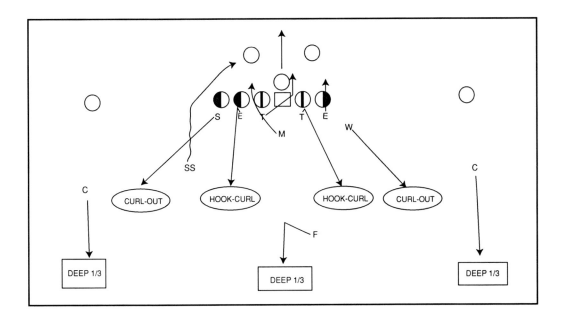

COACHING POINTS:

- This is a variation of **Cover 3 solid** that employs a **strong safety blitz**.

- The front is a balanced variation of a pro 4-3.

- This stunt incorporates **zone blitz** principles. As the quarterback approaches the center, the strong safety will move toward the line of scrimmage and blitz hard on an outside contain rush. Sam will line up in a 9 technique, control the D gap, and drop CURL-OUT versus pass. The strong end will line up in a 5 technique, control the C gap, and drop HOOK-CURL versus pass. The strong tackle will line up in a 2 technique, slant hard into the center, and attempt to crush the center into the weakside A gap. Mike will blitz the B gap. The weak tackle will line up in a 2 technique, control the B gap, and drop HOOK-CURL versus pass. The weak end will line up in a 5 technique, control the C gap, and contain the quarterback. The Will will contain weakside runs and drop CURL-OUT versus pass.

- Will and Sam are responsible for cutback.

STUNT #84

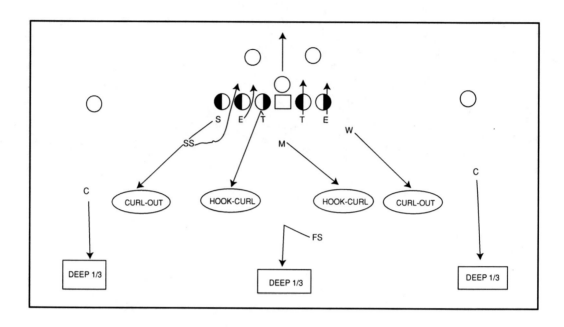

COACHING POINTS:

- This a is variation of **Cover 3 solid** that employs a **strong safety blitz**.

- The front is a balanced variation of a pro 4-3.

- This stunt incorporates **zone blitz** principles. As the quarterback approaches the center, the strong safety will move inside and blitz through the outside shoulder of the offensive tackle; he will control the C gap and contain the quarterback. Sam will line up in a 9 technique, contain strongside runs, and drop CURL-OUT versus pass. The strong end will line up in a 5 technique and slant hard into the B gap. Both tackles will line up in 1 techniques and control the A gaps versus run. Versus pass, the strong tackles will drop HOOK-CURL. Mike will over-read runs and drop HOOK-CURL versus pass. The weak end will line up in a 5 technique, control the C gap, and contain the quarterback. The Will will contain weakside runs and drop CURL-OUT versus pass.

- Will and Sam are responsible for cutback.

STUNT #85

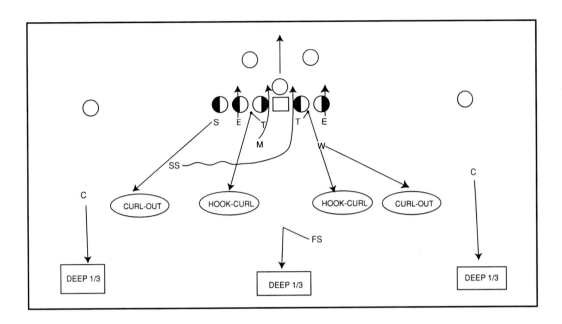

COACHING POINTS:

- This is variation of **Cover 3 solid** that employs a **strong safety blitz**.

- The front is an unbalanced variation of a pro 4-3.

- This is a **zone blitz**. As the quarterback approaches the center, the strong safety will move inside and blitz through the weakside A gap. Sam will line up in a 9 technique, contain strongside runs, and drop CURL-OUT versus pass. The strong end will line up in a 5 technique, control the C gap, and contain the quarterback. Both tackles will line up in 1 techniques. Although they will not flex, the tackles must back off the ball slightly. At the snap of the ball, the two tackles will slant into the B gaps and control these gaps versus run. Versus pass, they will both drop HOOK-CURL. Mike will blitz the strongside A gap. The weak end will line up in a 5 technique, control the C gap, and contain the quarterback. Will will over-read runs and drop CURL-OUT versus pass.

- Will and Sam are responsible for cutback.

CHAPTER 6

STUNTS FOR ADDITIONAL COVERAGES

This final chapter includes stunts for the following six coverages:

- Quarter/quarter/halves

- 2 strong/man weak

- Double Z Banjo

- Double X (Lock)

- Double X (Banjo)

- Robber

QUARTER/QUARTER HALF-COVERAGE

In this coverage, the strong cornerback and strong safety will defend the deep quarters of the field, and the free safety and the weak cornerback will employ the same techniques and reads that they did in 2 zone. The defenders dropping into the under coverage will play zone. If Sam, Mike, and Will were dropping into coverage, Sam would drop CURL-OUT, Mike would drop HOOK-CURL, and Will would drop HOOK-CURL.

The following diagram illustrates these assignments:

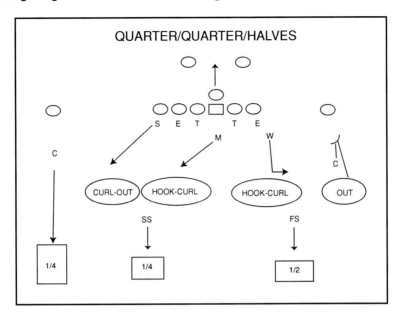

2 STRONG/MAN WEAK COVERAGE

Everyone will play 2 zone in this coverage except the weak cornerback; he will play man. The assignments for this coverage are illustrated in the following diagram:

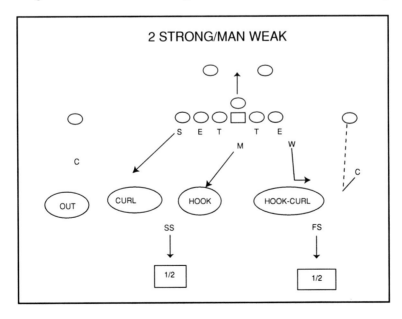

DOUBLE Z COVERAGE

This is a man coverage in which two defenders will cover the flanker, a safety will be free, and the under coverage will Banjo. The following assignments apply. The two cornerbacks will play man. The strong cornerback will aggressively attack the flanker, funnel him outside, and employ a trail technique. The weak cornerback will play a loose man technique. The strong safety will also cover the flanker, but he will play over the top. The free safety is free; Sam and Mike will Banjo the tight end and strongside halfback; and Will will cover the weakside halfback man-to-man. The following diagram illustrates these assignments:

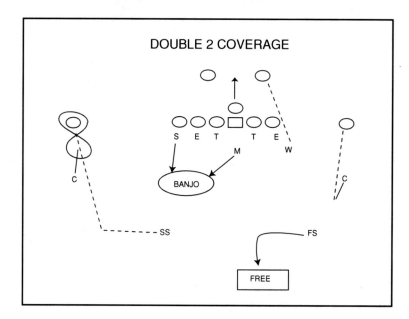

DOUBLE 2 COVERAGE

DOUBLE X LOCK COVERAGE

This is a man coverage in which two defenders will cover the split end, the strong safety will cover the tight end, and two defenders (linebackers or defensive linemen) will cover/spy the two running backs. An example of these assignments is as follows: The two cornerbacks will play man. The weak cornerback will aggressively attack the split end, funnel him outside, and employ a trail technique. The free safety will also cover the split end, but he will play over the top. The strong cornerback will play a loose man technique. The strong safety will cover the tight end; Sam will rush; and the Mike and Will will cover the near backs. The following diagram illustrates these assignments:

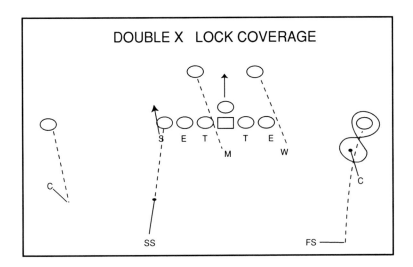

DOUBLE X LOCK COVERAGE

DOUBLE X BANJO COVERAGE

This is a man coverage in which two defenders will cover the split end, a safety will be free, and the under coverage will Banjo. The following assignments apply in this situation. The two cornerbacks will play man. The weak cornerback will aggressively attack the split end, funnel him outside, and employ a trail technique. The strong cornerback will play a loose man technique. The free safety will also cover the split end, but he will play over the top. The strong safety is free; Sam and Mike will Banjo the tight end and strong side halfback; and Will will cover the weakside halfback man-to-man. The following diagram illustrates these assignments:

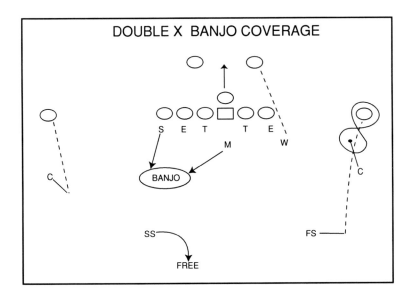

DOUBLE X BANJO COVERAGE

ROBBER COVERAGE

Many variations of robber coverage are being played today. My favorite variation is one in which the free safety is the robber He will rotate to the hole, rob crossing routes, and stop cutback. The strong safety is free in this coverage, and the under coverage will either Banjo or Lock. The following two diagrams illustrate an example of both Robber Banjo and Robber Lock:

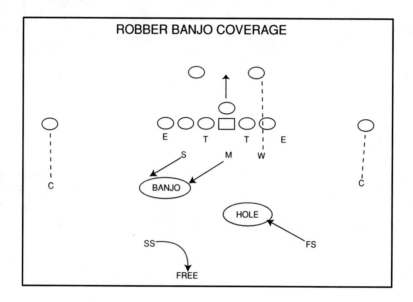

ROBBER BANJO COVERAGE

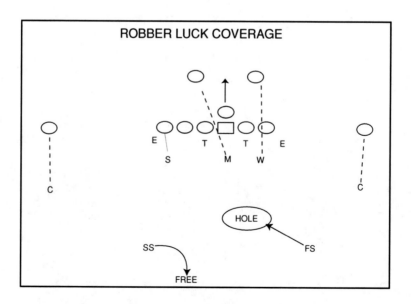

ROBBER LUCK COVERAGE

STUNT #86

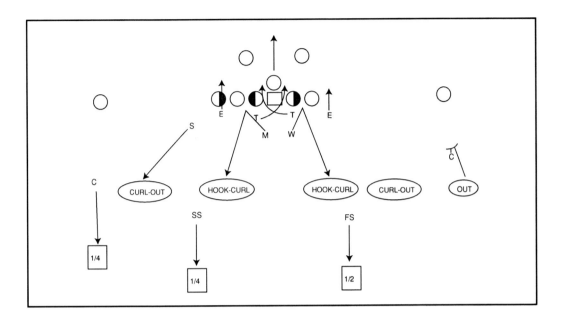

COACHING POINTS:

- This is a **quarter/quarter/halves** stunt.

- The front is an unbalanced variation of the 4-3 that gives the offense a split look.

- Sam will line up in a loose 8 technique, contain strongside runs, and drop CURL-OUT versus pass. The strong end will line up in a 7 technique, control the C gap, and contain the quarterback. Both tackles will line up in 3 techniques and twist into the A gaps. Will and Mike will scrape into the B gaps and control these gaps versus run; against pass, they will both drop HOOK-CURL. The weak end will line up in a 7 technique, control the C gap, and contain the quarterback.

- Will and Sam are responsible for cutback.

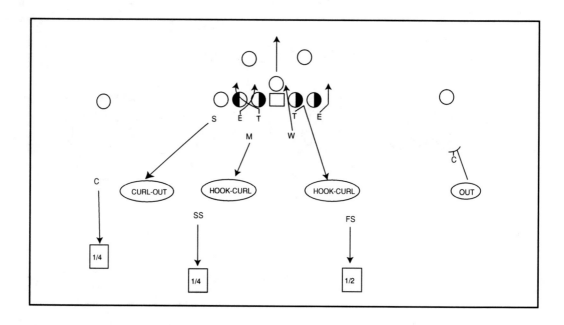

COACHING POINTS:

- This is a **quarter/quarter/halves** stunt.

- The front is an unbalanced variation (load or reduction) of the 4-3.

- This line twist is a delayed reaction to pass. Sam will line up in a 9 technique, contain strongside runs, and drop CURL-OUT versus pass. The strong end will line up in a 5 technique and control the C gap versus run. Versus pass, the strong end will engage the offensive tackle's block and then vigorously slant into the B gap. The strong tackle will line up in a 1 technique and control the A gap versus run; against pass, he will engage the offensive guard's block and then slant hard toward the weak offensive tackle's face and contain the quarterback. Mike will under-read run and drop HOOK-CURL versus pass. The Will will blitz the A gap. The weak tackle will line up in a 3 technique, control the B gap versus run, and drop HOOK-CURL versus pass. The weak end will line up in a 5 technique, slant outside, and contain the quarterback and weakside runs.

- Sam and the defenders filling gaps are responsible for cutback.

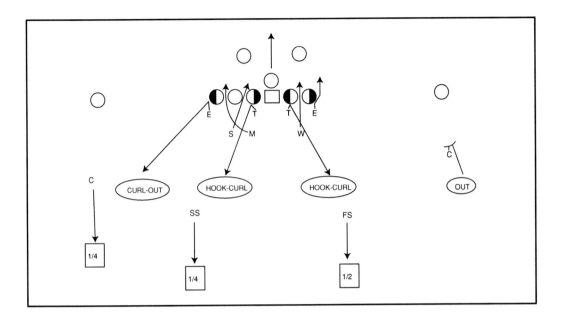

COACHING POINTS:

- This is a **quarter/quarter/halves** stunt.

- The front is an unbalanced variation of a college 4-3.

- This is a zone blitz. Sam will line up in a flexed 7 technique and blitz through the B gap. The strong end will line up in a 9 technique, control the D gap, and drop CURL-OUT versus pass. Mike will blitz the C gap and contain the quarterback. Both tackles will line up in 1 techniques, control the A gaps versus run, and drop HOOK-CURL versus pass. The Will will blitz the B gap. The weak end will line up in a 5 technique, control the C gap, and contain the quarterback.

- The defenders filling gaps are responsible for cutback.

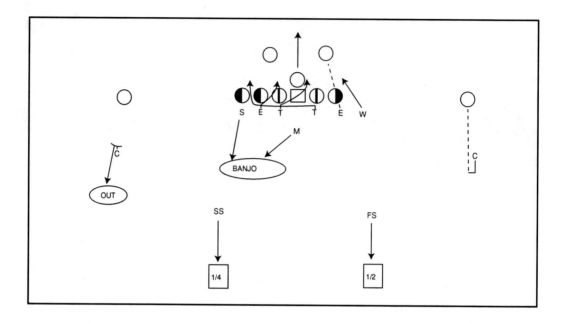

COACHING POINTS:

- This is a **2 strong/man weak coverage** stunt.

- The front is a balanced variation of the pro 4-3.

- This line twist is a delayed reaction to pass. Sam will line up in a 9 technique, contain strongside runs, and drop CURL-OUT versus pass. The strong end will line up in a 5 technique and control the C gap versus run. Versus pass, the strong end will engage the offensive tackle's block and then slant hard into the B gap. The strong tackle will line up in a 2 technique and control the B gap versus run; against pass, he will engage the offensive guard's block and then slant across the center's face into the weakside A gap. The weak tackle will line up in a 2 technique and control the B gap versus run; against pass, he will loop across the strong offensive tackle's face and contain the quarterback. The weak end will line up in a 5 technique, control the C gap versus run, and spy the near back. Mike will over-read run and Banjo drop-back action. Will is on a hard contain rush from the outside.

- Sam is responsible for cutback.

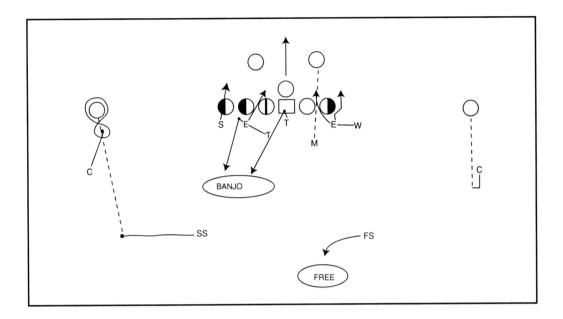

COACHING POINTS:

- This is a **double Z Banjo coverage** stunt.

- The front is a balanced (over) variation of the pro 4-3 in which the strong tackle is flexed.

- Sam will line up in a 9 technique and stunt on a contain rush. The strong end and tackle will twist. The strong tackle will drop off into Banjo coverage versus pass. The weak tackle will line up in a 0 technique and control both A gaps; versus pass, he will drop off into Banjo coverage. The weak end will stunt outside and contain the quarterback on pass. The Will will stunt into the B gap. Mike will over-read and cover the near back versus pass.

- Mike is responsible for cutback.

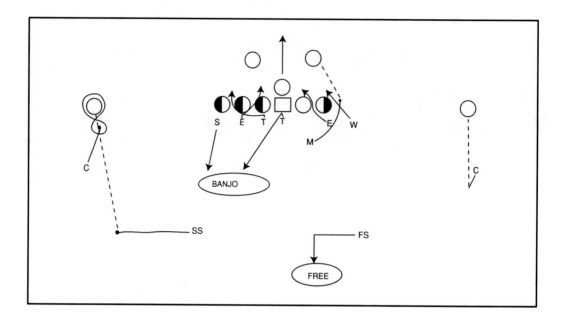

COACHING POINTS:

- This is a **double Z Banjo coverage** stunt

- The front is a balanced (over) variation of the pro 4-3.

- This strongside line twist is a delayed reaction to pass. Sam will line up in a 9 technique, contain strongside runs, and drop off into Banjo coverage versus pass. The strong end will line up in a 5 technique and control the C gap versus run. Versus pass, the strong end will engage the offensive tackle's block and then slant hard into the B gap. The strong tackle will line up in a 3 technique and control the B gap versus run; against pass, he will engage the offensive guard's block and then slant across the offensive tackle's face and contain the quarterback. The weak tackle will line up in a 0 technique and control both A gaps; versus pass, he will drop into Banjo coverage. The weak end will line up in a 5 technique and slant into the B gap. The Will will slant at the offensive tackle's heels, control the C gap, and contain the quarterback. Mike will stunt outside, contain weakside running plays, and spy the near back versus pass.

- Mike and Sam are responsible for cutback.

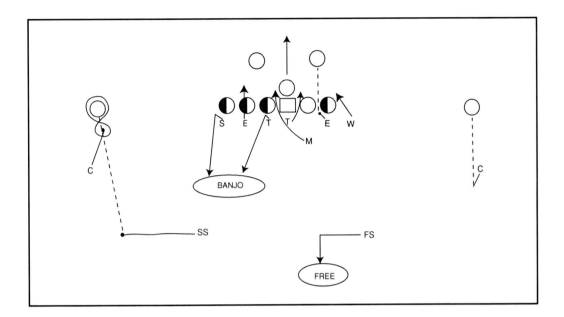

COACHING POINTS:

- This is a **double Z Banjo coverage** stunt.

- The front is a balanced (over) variation of the pro 4-3.

- Sam will line up in a 9 technique, contain strongside runs, and drop off into Banjo coverage versus pass. The strong end will line up in a 5 technique, control the C gap, and contain the quarterback versus pass. The strong tackle will line up in a 3 technique and control the B gap; versus pass, he will drop off into Banjo coverage. The weak tackle will line up in a 0 technique and slant into the weakside A gap. The weak end will line up on the inside shoulder of the offensive tackle, control the B gap, and spy the near back. The Will will slant at the offensive tackle's heels, control the C gap, and contain the quarterback. Mike will blitz the strongside A gap.

- Sam and the defenders filling gaps are responsible for cutback.

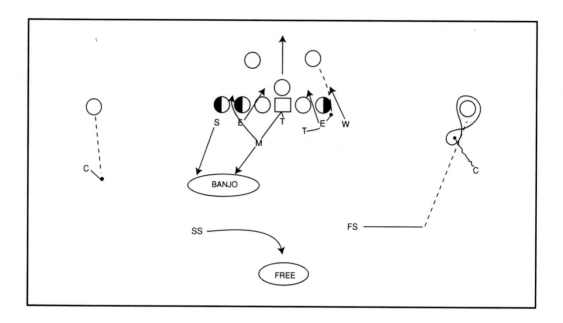

COACHING POINTS:

• This is a **double X Banjo coverage** stunt.

• The front is a balanced (under) variation of the pro 4-3 in which the weak tackle is flexed.

• Sam will line up in a 9 technique, contain strongside runs, and drop off into Banjo coverage versus pass. The strong end and Mike will twist; Mike is responsible for containment versus pass. The strong tackle will line up in a 0 technique and control both A gaps; versus pass, he will drop off into Banjo coverage. The weak tackle and weak end will twist; versus pass, the weak tackle will spy the near back. The Will will rush hard from the outside and contain weakside runs and passes.

• Sam and the defenders filling gaps are responsible for cutback.

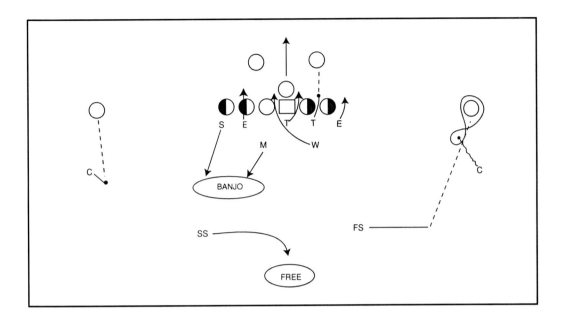

COACHING POINTS:

- This is a **double X Banjo coverage** stunt.

- The front is a balanced (under) variation of the pro 4-3.

- Sam will line up in a 9 technique, contain strongside runs, and drop off into Banjo coverage versus pass. The strong end will line up in a 5 technique, control the C gap, and contain the quarterback. Mike will control the B gap and drop off into Banjo coverage versus pass. The strong tackle will line up in a 0 technique and slant into the weakside A gap. The weak tackle will line up in a 3 technique, slant into the B gap, and spy the near back. The Will will blitz through the strongside A gap. The weak end will line up in a 5 technique, slant outside, and contain weakside runs and the quarterback.

- Sam and Mike are responsible for cutback.

STUNT #95

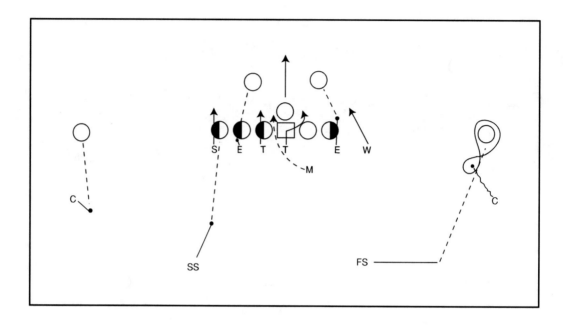

COACHING POINTS:

- This is a **double X lock coverage** stunt.

- The front is a balanced (over) variation of the pro 4-3.

- Sam will line up in a 9 technique, rush hard from the outside, and contain the quarterback and strongside runs. The strong end will line up in a 5 technique, control the C gap, and spy the near back. The strong tackle will line up in a 3 technique and control the B gap. The weak tackle will line up in a 0 technique and control both A gaps. Versus the pass, the weak tackle will engage the center and then rush hard through the weakside A gap. It is the weak tackle's responsibility to make certain that the center can't block Mike. Mike will control the weakside B gap versus run. Against pass, Mike will delay blitz through the strongside A gap. The weak end will line up in a 5 technique, control the C gap, and spy the near back. The Will will rush hard from the outside and contain the quarterback and weakside runs.

- Sam and Mike are responsible for cutback.

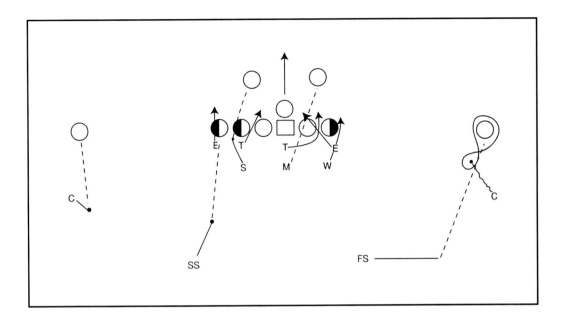

COACHING POINTS:

- This is a **double X lock coverage** stunt.

- The front is a (Kansas City stack) variation of the pro 4-3.

- The strong end will line up in a 9 technique, control the D gap, and contain pass. The strong tackle will slant into the B gap. Sam will fake a blitz through the outside shoulder of the offensive tackle, control the C gap, and spy the near back. Mike will control both A gaps and cover the near back. The weak end will line up in a 5 technique and slant through the outside shoulder of the offensive guard. The weak tackle will line up in a 0 technique and loop into the B gap. The Will will blitz through the outside shoulder of the offensive tackle, control the C gap, and contain the quarterback.

- Sam and the defenders filling gaps are responsible for cutback.

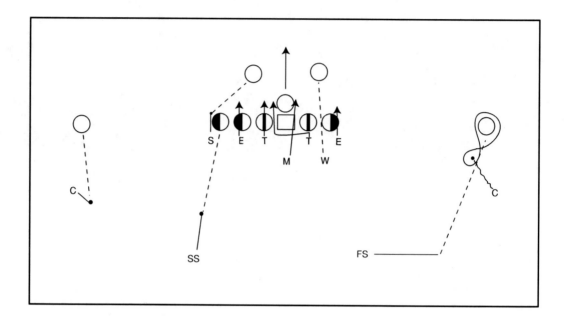

COACHING POINTS:

- This is a **double X lock coverage** stunt that is excellent versus pass.

- The front is a balanced variation of the pro 4-3.

- Sam will line up in a 9 technique, control the D gap, and spy the near back. The strong tackle will line up in a 5 technique, control the C gap, and contain pass. The strong tackle will line up in a 2 technique and control the B gap. Mike will blitz through the weakside shoulder of the center. The weak tackle will draw the guard's block, wait for Mike to clear, and then loop into the strongside A gap. The Will will under-read run and cover the near back. The weak end will line up in a 5 technique, control the C gap, and contain the quarterback

- Sam and Will are responsible for cutback.

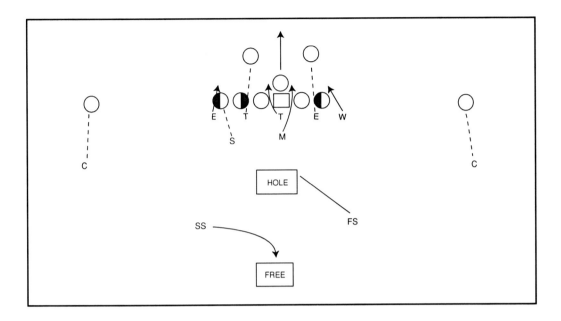

COACHING POINTS:

- This is a **robber lock coverage** stunt.

- The front is a variation of the pro 4-3 that resembles the Kansas City stack.

- The strong end will line up in a 9 technique, control the D gap, and contain pass. The strong tackle will line up on the inside shoulder of the offensive tackle, control the B gap, and spy the near back. Mike and the weak tackle will blitz into the A gaps. The weak end will line up on the inside shoulder of the offensive tackle, control the B gap, and spy the near back. The Will will rush hard from the outside and contain weakside run and pass.

- The free safety is responsible for cutback.

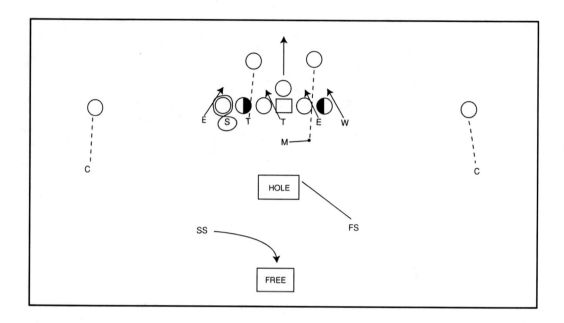

COACHING POINTS:

- This is a **robber lock coverage** stunt.

- The front is a variation of the pro 4-3 that resembles the Kansas City stack.

- The strong end will line up in an 8 technique and crash hard, containing pass and run. Sam will line up in a 7 technique and cover the tight end. The strong tackle will line up on the inside shoulder of the offensive tackle, control the B gap, and spy the near back. Mike will over-read, check the weakside A gap, and cover the near back. The weak tackle will slant into the A gap. The weak end will line up on the inside shoulder of the offensive tackle and slant into the B gap. The Will will rush hard at the heels of the offensive tackle, control the C gap, and contain the quarterback.

- The free safety is responsible for cutback.

STUNT #100

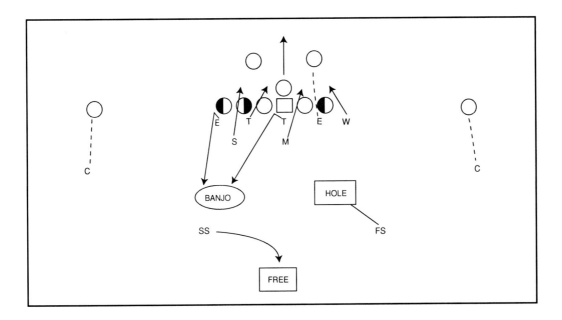

COACHING POINTS:

- This is a **robber Banjo coverage** stunt.

- The front is a variation of the pro 4-3 that resembles the Kansas City stack.

- The strong end will line up in an 9 technique, control the D gap, and drop into Banjo coverage versus pass. Sam will blitz through the outside shoulder of the offensive tackle. The strong tackle will line up on the inside shoulder of the offensive tackle and slant into the B gap. Mike will blitz through the weakside A gap. The weak tackle will slant into the strongside A gap and drop off into Banjo coverage versus pass. The weak end will line up on the inside shoulder of the offensive tackle, control the B gap, and spy the near back. The Will will control the C gap and contain the quarterback.

- The free safety is responsible for cutback.

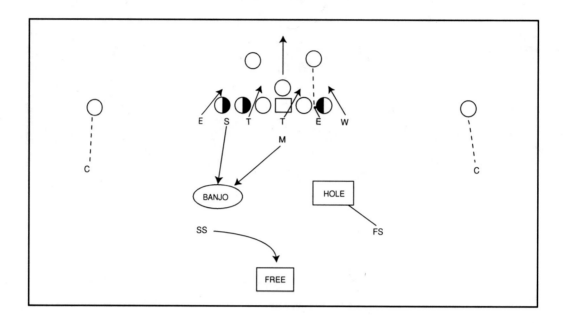

COACHING POINTS:

- This is a **robber Banjo coverage** stunt.

- The front is a variation of the pro 4-3 that resembles the Kansas City stack.

- The strong end will line up in an 8 technique and crash hard, containing pass and run. Sam will line up in a 7 technique, control the C gap, and drop off into Banjo coverage. The strong tackle will line up on the inside shoulder of the offensive tackle and slant into the B gap. Mike will over-read run and cover the near back. The weak tackle will line up in a 0 technique and slant into the weakside A gap. The weak end will line up on the inside shoulder of the offensive tackle, control the B gap, and spy the near back. The Will will rush hard at the heels of the offensive tackle, control the C gap, and contain the quarterback.

- The free safety is responsible for cutback.

Leo Hand is the defensive coordinator at El Paso (TX) High School, a position he assumed in 2001. Prior to that, he held the same job at Irvin High School in El Paso, Texas. With over 33 years of experience as a teacher and coach, Hand has served in a variety of coaching positions in his career. At each stop, he has achieved a notable level of success.

A graduate of Emporia State University in Emporia, Kansas, Hand began his football coaching career in 1968 as the junior varsity coach at McQuaid Jesuit High School in Rochester, New York. After two seasons, he then accepted the job as the offensive line coach at Aquinas Institute (1970-'71). Next, he served as the head coach at Saint John Fisher College — a position he held for two years. He has also served on the gridiron staffs at APW (Parrish, NY) High School (head coach); Saint Anthony (Long Beach, CA) High School (head coach), Daniel Murphy (Los Angeles, CA) High School (head coach), Servite (Anaheim, CA) High School (head coach); Serra (Gardena, CA) High School (head coach); Long Beach (CA) City College (offensive line and linebackers); and Los Angeles (CA) Harbor College (offensive coordinator).

During the six-year period he spent coaching interscholastic teams in California, his squads won 81 percent of their games in the highly competitive area of Southern California. At Serra High School, his team compiled a 24-1 record, won a CIF championship, and were declared California State champions. On numerous occasions, he has helped rebuild several floundering gridiron teams into highly successful programs. For his efforts, he has been honored on numerous occasions with Coach-of-the-Year recognition.

A former golden gloves boxing champion, he is a prolific author, having written several football instructional books and numerous articles that have been published. He and his wife, Mary, have nine children and seven grandchildren.